it's a
BREAKUP *not a*
BREAKDOWN

it's a BREAKUP not a BREAKDOWN

Get over the big one and change your life—for good!

lisa **steadman**

POLKA DOT press.

avon, massachusetts

The Polka Dot Press® name and logo design are registered trademarks
of F+W Publications, Inc.

Published by Polka Dot Press,
an imprint of Adams Media, an F+W Publications Company
57 Littlefield Street, Avon, MA 02322 U.S.A.
www.adamsmedia.com

ISBN-10: 1-59869-172-4
ISBN-13: 978-1-59869-172-6

Printed in the United States of America.

J I H G F E D C B

Library of Congress Cataloging-in-Publication Data

Steadman, Lisa.
It's a breakup, not a breakdown / Lisa Steadman.
p.   cm.
ISBN-13: 978-1-59869-172-6 (pbk.)
ISBN-10: 1-59869-172-4 (pbk.)
1. Man-woman relationships—Anecdotes. 2. Dating (Social
customs)—Anecdotes. 3. Mate selection—Anecdotes. I. Title.
HQ801.S793 2007
646.7'7—dc22   2007001127

*This book is available at quantity discounts for bulk purchases.
For information, please call 1-800-289-0963.*

Dedication

For every woman who has ever been through a Big Breakup and the sisterhood of fabulous females who always helps us heal.

And to my own amazingly supportive Boo-Hoo Crew:

My sister Staci, who's seen me through every breakup I've *ever* had

Lani, who's been my constant cheerleader through all the L.A. breakups

Eve, for encouraging me to never settle for less than I deserve

Gretchen, for believing in my Fabulous Factor even when I didn't

Negin, for the sleepovers, wine, and lunches at the beach following my Big Breakup

Melanie, for my *Aha!* moment in her living room after the Big Breakup

Karraine, my fellow Montana adventure girl, for our unspoken pact to once again open our hearts

And to my mom, for always supporting my breakup choices

You ladies ROCK!

contents

Preface

When the idea first came to me to write about breakups, I was in the throes of my own Big Breakup. And boy, was it messy! I had spent the last six months breaking up and then making up with Mr. Ex, not once but many times. By the time all was said and done, I was a big fat screaming mess. I cried myself to sleep every night. Actually, I cried when I woke up in the morning, cried when I took a shower, cried on my way to work, cried in the bathroom at work, cried to my girlfriends on the phone, cried on the way home from work, cried on my couch at night, and *then* cried myself to sleep.

I knew this was my Big Breakup because of how it felt. Or rather, how it made me feel—completely crushed. It was as if my ex's giant foot had stomped on me, flattening me like a pancake. I'd been through breakups before, but nothing had prepared me for this. Walking and breathing barely felt possible, let alone the effort of trying to function like a normal human being.

But even though I was in tremendous pain, I knew it was for the best. Deep down, I knew Mr. Ex wasn't right for me. As much as I wanted him to be The One, there had always been plenty of evidence that he wasn't (the mood swings, his controlling father, those nagging money problems). I knew that the sooner I accepted this, the better off I'd be. Still, I resisted. I thought Mr. Ex brought something to my life that was otherwise missing. I thought he held the key to my fabulousness. In breaking up with Mr. Ex, I thought, I was no longer special.

I was wrong.

Somewhere amidst all the crying, moping, and self-pity, I realized that Mr. Ex didn't hold the key to what made me fabulous. Even with my puffy eyes and broken heart, I was still pretty magnificent. I just had some healing to do and some stuff to figure out—like why I thought I needed Mr. Ex to make me feel good. It was then that I decided I didn't want to fall in love again until I had made peace with my own issues and insecurities. After all, my Big Breakup wasn't exactly my first breakup. If I didn't learn my lessons and make some much-needed changes, it wouldn't be my last, either. And so I decided to make use of my pain by writing about it. I started asking my friends to share their breakup stories with me as well. I called these stories *The Breakup Chronicles*.

What started as a book idea turned into a column, which eventually, at the advice of a very patient newspaper editor, became my Web site, *www.breakupchronicles.com*. Launched in August of 2004, BreakupChronicles.com was nothing more than a pet project with big dreams of reaching Oprah, Dr. Phil, and Jennifer Lopez (these were the Diddy days). And while my initial ambitions weren't realized, what happened instead was far better. Real people began sharing their breakup stories and the lessons learned. In reading other people's stories, I began to see a common thread—that as difficult as breakups both big and small are, they always teach us something valuable.

For me, all the little breakups that came before my Big Breakup were like subtle nudges trying to clue me in to my own destructive relationship behavior. Like the fact that I expected a man to fix me. Or that I somehow thought *some guy* could make me happy when I wasn't happy on my own. Or the fact that I had impossibly high expectations of my relationships and yet chose wildly inappropriate partners who were incapable of meeting those expectations. And yet somehow I acted surprised when I continually stumbled over the same relationship ruts again and again. Being the stubborn Libra that I am, I did my best to ignore the lessons my little breakups were trying to teach me. Which is why The Big Breakup didn't take any chances. No, it made itself known loud and clear. It changed everything. The Big Breakup was especially significant to me—and it can be to you, too—because it was the one that told me exactly what I needed to hear. It was the one that said, *This is the way to your authentic life, but it's up to you to follow.*

After my Big Breakup (and all the pain that came along with it), I decided to take that bold leap and follow my authentic life path. I left a good job for a better life. Not long after my big leap, I launched my site and started getting paid to write about dating and relationships (and breakups, of course!). As time went on, people started calling. No, not Oprah or Dr. Phil. But *The Tyra Banks Show* sent a limo for me once. I was invited to be a guest on various radio and television shows to talk about the positive side of breaking up. I even found a publisher. Actually, she found me. And when her bosses turned down our book idea, she sent me to an editor whose bosses didn't. (Thanks, Danielle and Jennifer!)

And just as rewarding as this new career path was, my personal life benefited greatly, too. After taking some much-needed time off, I started dating again. A lot. (I highly recommend it!) I met some interesting guys and some not-so-interesting ones, too. Some of them thought the breakup stuff was cool. Others were intimidated, worried that I was using them for research. And that was fine. They quickly faded into obscurity.

Somewhere in all this dating I fell in love—with my new life. I realized that while I still hoped one day to find real and lasting love, the life I was leading in the meantime was fantastic! In some ways, that was what I'd been looking for all along—happiness that came from within. I didn't need a man to fulfill me. I found new and meaningful ways to lead a fulfilling life on my own terms.

Then, one night when I least expected it, I met Mr. XY. Like me, he was healthy and whole and happy being alone. He, too, had been through his Big Breakup and had decided that he wasn't going to fall in love again until he'd made peace with his own issues. Midway through our first date, I realized this man was different and I'd be a fool not to get to know him. He said that by our second date he knew we'd eventually fall in love. Three months later, we were living together. It just felt right. And as I write this today on our living room couch, I can't get over how amazing our relationship is or how lucky I feel. By the time you read this, we will have been together for almost two years.

I tell you about Mr. XY not because I think it makes me any more qualified to write this book. I would've written this book with or without Mr. XY. But I tell you about him because he *is* significant to this book. If it hadn't been for my Big Breakup, for all the lessons I learned from my own stories and from other people's stories, and the incredible journey I've been on, I never would have or could have seen Mr. XY for the amazing, loving, whole individual that he is. And he never would have given me the time of day had I stayed the big fat screaming mess I was after my Big Breakup. So I tell you about Mr. XY (1) to give thanks to everyone who's shared their story with me and helped me heal, and (2) to illustrate the value of moving on after breakups both big and small. There *is* life after all the pain. It *does* get better.

You just have to have a little faith. Well, you have to be willing to work through the pain, give yourself permission to heal and move on, *and* have a little faith. That's what this book is all about.

Thank you for picking up *It's a BreakUP, Not a Breakdown.* Regardless of whether this is your Big Breakup or one of your many breakup nudges along the way, I look forward to helping you through it. Together, we will survive and thrive!

Introduction

Congratulations on your breakup.

Nobody ever says that, do they?

But they should.

Let me say it again.

Congratulations on your breakup!

See, I added an exclamation point this time because it really is *big*. All breakups are significant in some way because of what they ultimately teach us about ourselves. And the Big Breakup is especially significant. If you're going through it, then you know what I'm talking about. The relationship was big. The breakup was definitely big. The resulting pain is big. Maybe even the relief is big. And I've got news for you—the movin' on is really B-I-G. Regardless of whether your most recent breakup was big or small (or somewhere in between), there's plenty to learn from the experience. Now's the time to realize that it's not called a breakup because you're breaking down. It's called a breakup because you're breaking *up* with a relationship that's no longer working and moving *on* to a life better suited for you. Even if you were the one who got broken up with, you now have the chance to move onward and upward. It won't always be easy. After all, we're talking about a breakup, and that's never easy. But don't worry—it's not all pain and anguish. Sure, breakups are painful, but they're also freeing and fabulous because they free us *up* to be our most *fabulous* selves.

If you're going through a breakup, you may think your life will never be the same again. I've got news for you—it won't. But that's fantastic! The truth is all breakups change us in some way. And the Big Breakup changes everything. Mine did and yours will, too. I'm not saying your breakup will cause you to make drastic and unnecessary changes to your life, but it will most likely make you look at your life in a new light. It will bring up some inevitable questions: *What do I want to do now? What really makes me happy?* I think you'll be surprised by the answers that come to you.

Today you may be feeling empowered and healthy about your breakup. Or you may be filled with doubt, despair, and confusion. Don't worry. During your post-breakup recovery, you'll most likely feel like you're on an emotional roller coaster. You'll go back and forth many times between the two extremes before you fully move on. That's perfectly normal. Just ride it out. Trust that you will get through this and that you'll be stronger for doing so. You *will* survive and even thrive without Mr. Ex. Regardless of how you're feeling right now, you are not broken. Your heart may feel like it's been shattered into a trillion tiny pieces, but it's still there. It's still beating. It still loves you. It still believes in love. (It just needs a little time to heal first.)

There are breakup books that tell you not to call that man. Books that say he's just not that into you. Books that toy with revenge tactics. *It's a BreakUP, Not a Breakdown* is a different kind of breakup book. It's a step-by-step guide to getting over your Big Breakup.

In Part One, you'll get a crash course in breakup survival—the good, the bad, the oh-so-ugly. I'll share the lessons others have shared with me through my Web site, *www.breakupchronicles.com*. And of course I'll tell you about my Big Breakup—The One That Rocked My World for a good six months (okay, a year) after our second official breakup. Yup, I had to break up with Mr. Ex not once but twice to learn my lesson. But you know what? After all that pain, my heart did heal. And yours will, too. Maybe that seems impossible right now, but it's the fabulous truth.

When you're ready, we'll move on to Part Two of this book, which starts with a movin' on party to celebrate the life that's waiting for you now that you've lost 170-plus pounds of excess weight (also known as Mr. Ex). It's the quickest weight loss plan in history! After the party, we'll get back to the business of you and your fabulous new life. From making over your space to falling in love with your life to dating and eventually falling in love with someone new, Part Two is all about shaking things up as you move on post-breakup. Even if this wasn't your Big Breakup—if, say, you're recovering from breakup number six in as many months—don't worry. You'll find what you need in these pages, too.

But for now, let's get back to you and your breakup. You may be thinking nobody knows what you're going through. That nobody knows how hard this is. I'm here to remind you it's not true. I'm here to give you a big fat medal for just making it through the day. (Seriously, turn to the back of the book. There's a Breakup Survivor Medal just for you!)

I'm also here to welcome you to the rest of your life. It's a life full of amazing adventures, should you choose them. You no longer have to settle for less than you deserve or put up with someone else's unclaimed baggage.

I have a secret for you: There's someone out there who's better suited for you. When the time is right, you can have the relationship you truly deserve—a happy, healthy, whole one. But you first have to give yourself permission to wake up, break up, and move on. And that's what this book is about.

At this point, it's time to say it once again:

Congratulations on your breakup!!!

And this time, I ask you to join me. Say it loud, say it proud:

"*congratulations* on your (my) breakup!!!"

Didn't that feel good?

Okay, you may be thinking. *That did feel kind of good. But now what?*

I'll tell you what now.

You are now ready to get down to the business of recovering from your Big Breakup. Soon you'll know what other breakup survivors know—that this breakup is one of the best things that will ever happen to you. One day in the not-too-distant future, you'll be minding your own business, actively involved in your amazing life, and it will hit you—*I'm over him*. And not only that, your next thought will be *Thank God he got away!*

It's okay not to be there yet. It takes time. And we've got all the time in the world. After all, this is your life; nothing's more important than getting you through this. Don't think of your breakup as a breakdown. Think breaking *up*. It's now time to break *up* and move on. (Don't worry—I'll show you how!)

breakingUP

Wise Words from The Breakup Chronicles:

"I thought that I would never live again. Or laugh. Or feel joy. I thought that when he left, he took those parts of me with him. Now I know better. Now I see him for who he is, and more importantly, I see myself. For the first time in a long time, I see myself. And I love her. She's a fighter."

—Nadine

A Year at a Glance

everyone knows there's no such thing as a good time to break up. But some times are definitely more appropriate than others. The following sections outline some of the best—and absolute worst—times to break up throughout the year. See where your own breakup fits in. Were you set free in the spring? Split by September? Or dumped in December? Regardless of when the breakup happened, let me be the first to say it: *Congratulations!*

Best-Case-Scenario Breakup Dates: March to August

Spring and summer are optimal breakup seasons. Regardless of where you live, chances are that the gloomy winter weather has disappeared and the sun is shining when you get dumped (or do the dumping). Breakup etiquette experts agree. If your relationship isn't working, and you know you gotta end it eventually, dumping someone during this time period is not only considerate, it's encouraged!

If your ex gave you the boot during these dump-friendly months, consider yourself lucky. He probably knew what you, too, soon will know, that it's hard to stay depressed when the sun doesn't set until late and there are healthy, happy, hot singles everywhere you go. You might even say he did you a favor in cutting you loose because now you're free to heal your heart and enjoy a "single and ready to mingle" summer. So buck up, Brokenhearted, and be open to the endless possibilities that now await you.

In the meantime, curl up with this book and let the healing begin!

Last-Resort Breakup Dates: September to Early November

Did the spring and summer fly by without so much as a hint of dating drama? Or were you on a relationship roller coaster, suffering silently until you just couldn't take it anymore? Chances are good that at some point during the last few months (or longer, if your relationship was dying a slow death), things have been rocky. Either you or your ex knew in your heart of hearts that the two of you weren't going to make it as a couple. And rather than suffer through the fall, endure a difficult holiday season, and barely make it to Valentine's Day without killing each other, one or both of you consulted the breakup etiquette books and realized that it was just better to cut your losses before Thanksgiving than go through the motions until February. Regardless of who broke up with whom, these post-summer months are still an acceptable time to call it quits.

Whether you got the ax or did the dumping, if your breakup broke during this time period, you've got a lot to be thankful for. Like the fact that there's one less mouth to feed at Thanksgiving, a lot fewer presents to buy at Christmas, and no longer a need to kiss your slobbering ex on New Year's Eve. So dry your eyes, and get to work on healing your heart. You never know whom you might meet under the mistletoe this year. Very soon, you'll be giving thanks for the one who got away. (And in the meantime? Keep reading!)

Breakup Blackout Dates: Mid-November to Mid-February

Anyone who dumps someone during the holiday months is a total chump. The exception here is if you're dumping some cheating chump who desperately deserves it. Assuming that's not the case, only someone practicing bad breakup etiquette would wait until the breakup blackout dates to do the dumping. It's just bad form.

Having said that, if you happen to find yourself getting dumped during this time period, fear not. A little pity party can earn you extra Christmas gifts and maybe some giant-sized Tupperware filled with Mom's delicious holiday goodies to help ease your broken heart. Chances are good that by Valentine's Day, you will have practically forgotten your ex. (Now *that's* worth celebrating.) Or if you got dumped too close to Valentine's Day, don't spend February 14 crying over some creep who didn't deserve you. Instead, celebrate the fact that not only did the wrong guy get away, but soon enough you'll be ready, willing, and able to meet Mr. Right. (So hop to the healing!)

Post-Breakup Supply Checklist

Before you read any further, make sure you have all the post-breakup supplies you'll need:

○ Glass of wine or cup of hot tea
○ Comfy clothes
○ Favorite blanket or quilt
○ Box of tissues
○ A cozy couch, chair, or bed to curl up in

Now, settle in and get comfy. We're gonna get through this together.

CHAPTER ONE
welcome
to your breakUP

for the record, your breakup rocks. Why? Because you chose you—*amazing you*—over a relationship that wasn't working anymore. I think that's incredibly brave and inspiring. If you were the one who got broken up with, don't think that getting dumped means you're broken or that you don't rock. Maybe you hadn't yet worked up the courage to end things. Or maybe the whole breakup came as a shock. If it did, consider it a wakeup call (and a gift from the universe). Obviously, the person who broke up with you wasn't right for you. In ending your relationship, he just gave you permission to move on without looking like the villain. (Hey, that rocks, too!)

Look around for a minute. How many people do you think are staying in relationships that no longer work? I'm guessing a lot. And unlike you, they just haven't found the faith or courage to be honest with themselves and their partners and initiate the breakup.

What if your Big Breakup involved a ring, a registry, invitations, and/or the hiring and firing of a deejay or band? Regardless of who called off the engagement, canceled the wedding, or was left at the altar (or somewhere along the journey to it), you deserve a standing ovation. Chances are that you and/or your ex knew deep down that things were not going to work out. In the end, one or both of you did yourselves a huge favor in calling it quits *before* the actual wedding.

Of course that doesn't make the pain go away, does it? Nor does it do much to ease the guilt that comes with calling off an engagement or wedding. The best thing you can do right now is try not to get hung up on the details, like whether or not deposits are refundable or which family member is most devastated by the change in plans. This is your life. You deserve to live it the way you want. And whether you know it right now or not, calling off your nuptials was for the best. So give yourself permission to let go of any guilt you're feeling, and allow yourself to take some much-needed time to heal your heart. Together, we will get through this.

If you're going through a smaller breakup, don't worry. We, too, will get through it together. After all, breakups come in all shapes and sizes. Some happen after relationships that lasted for years—decades even. Some happen after just months. It's not important how long you were together or whether you exchanged vows, lived together, had children, or met each other's families. None of those details matter. The Big Breakup isn't about how the relationship looked to other people. It's about how it looked—and, more importantly, how it felt—to *you*. If it shook you to the core, stirred your soul, and made you feel like you'd been thrown from the eye of a storm, then yes. You've just been through your Big Breakup. And that rocks!

Why?

Because after the intense, agonizing, and/or nauseating pain comes the pleasure. (You heard me—the pleasure!) The pleasure of rediscovering yourself and your fabulous life. The pleasure of your girlfriends' company, who always help you heal. Even the pleasure of allowing yourself that cookie-dough ice cream every night for three weeks. Or three months. (Don't worry, you'll put the carton down when you're ready.) Eventually, you'll even get to the pleasure of meeting someone new. Someone better suited for you. Someone you never could have appreciated or loved without having gone through your Big Breakup and learned all those juicy life lessons (not to mention a few breakup secrets, which I'll share with you along the way).

FROM THE DEADBEAT BOYFRIEND FILES

Think your breakup was bad?
Check out what this clueless cad did . . .

" In the beginning, my ex was the sweetest person. After a year of being together, he started to change. He became suspicious of where I was going and who I was with. Then one day he came home and accused me of giving him an STD. I had never slept around on this man. My gut told me to go to the doctor and when I did, my worst fears were confirmed. My ex had given me an STD. *He* was cheating on *me*. I feel like such a fool!"

—*Beth*

Fortunately for Beth, her STD was treatable. But her ex better watch out—breakup karma is a bitch and it will find that clueless cad.

breakup secret #1

You're going to be just fine. In fact, you're going to be more than fine. You're going to be spectacular! That's because you're no longer in a relationship that's not working. You may not know it yet, but one day soon you'll be giving thanks for the one who got away.

The Agony vs. the Ecstasy

Now, just because your breakup rocks doesn't mean it doesn't hurt. It means that when you're hurting, you should remember that there's a light at the end of the tunnel. And no, it's not your ex on a bullet train hurtling toward you. It's the knowledge that something wonderful is going to come out of this pain. It's up to us to figure out what that something wonderful is and how it's going to shape the rest of your life.

RECOVERY ℞

To kick-start your breakup recovery, buy yourself a journal so that you can write about all of the things you're feeling right now. Don't worry, nobody's going to read it. This is just for you, so get as messy and mad as you want! I'll be asking you to write in your breakup recovery journal from time to time so keep it handy when you're reading this book. And feel free to cover it with images that make you happy (you can pull these from magazines and make a breakup recovery collage). You can also purchase a breakup recovery journal from The Breakup Chronicles at *www.cafepress.com/breakupshop*.

My good friend Lani, a writer and artist who was there for me during my Big Breakup, once described the difficult circumstances that led to her own bust-up with Mr. Wrong:

Here are my excuses: I was lonely, heartbroken, and lacking in self-esteem, self-worth and self-knowledge—not necessarily in that order. I didn't know what I wanted out of life, thought I had lost my youth, and had gained twenty pounds in two months. At such times in a woman's life she sees only one "cure," however temporary. That cure is sex. ✳

And while sex with Mr. Ex was a quick fix, it eventually wasn't enough to sustain their dead-end relationship. After months of drama, Lani woke up one morning to three inner truths that rocked her world:

I want better than this.

I deserve better than this.

I am better than this.

With that epiphany, Lani initiated her Big Breakup. Not long after that, she moved to California, where she met the husband to whom she has been happily married for years now. Without her Big Breakup, Lani would never have connected to those inner truths. She would never have been able to appreciate her sweet, stable husband if she hadn't already realized what she deserved in both life *and* love, thanks in part to Mr. Ex. And that's just it. When we know better, we do better. But until that time, we set ourselves up for all kinds of crazy relationships. Of course, they never seem impossibly crazy at the time. When my friend Jeff shared his Big Breakup story with me, he described how he dumped his down-to-earth girlfriend in favor of his ex, a woman more interested in looking cool than being real, only to later realize he'd made a terrible error in judgment:

Two weeks into our rekindled relationship, I found myself sitting outside a run-down tattoo shack in Hermosa

Beach. I was smoking again. Ms. Ex was inside getting "fresh ink." It was my turn next. It was then that I realized I didn't want a tattoo. I didn't want to be sitting outside, smoking and trying to be cool.

I got up and went inside to check on Ms. Ex. She had finished getting her "ink" and was sitting on the tattoo artist's lap, completely oblivious to the fact that I was outside waiting for her. It was then that I realized that I had been dumb to go back to this life. I flicked my "cool" cigarette to the floor, walked out, and never looked back. I have been a better person ever since. ✳

After Jeff's Big Breakup, he met and married an amazing woman and they now have a baby boy. Thank God he wised up and kicked his ex to the curb when he did. (It also goes to show that men go through their Big Breakups, too.)

Breakup Vocabulary

Ex Factor The status of your relationship with your most recent ex.

Boo-Hoo Crew A group of at least three girlfriends who are tasked with helping you get through your breakup. Part emotional babysitter, part tough-love drill sergeant, the Boo-Hoo Crew offers support, guidance, and general ex-boyfriend bashing (as needed).

Breakup Timeline A measuring tool to help determine one's progress after a breakup. The standard formula is Time + Distance = Moving on.

Ex Etiquette A set of rules regarding contact with an ex that should always be strictly adhered to after the breakup.

Fabulous Factor A list that every woman should create and carry, especially post-breakup, to remind herself of her own innate fabulousness.

PBT Post-breakup trauma. A temporary stress-related condition brought on by a breakup that can be used to explain erratic behavior like reckless rebounding, ridiculous revenge plots, and random fits of laughter followed by uncontrollable sobbing. (Don't worry—it's all perfectly normal.)

The Slump The mourning period following a breakup characterized by irrational outbursts, emotional eating/drinking/shopping, and a lack of interest in the world outside of the breakup.

Speaking of Exes

Now would be a good time to talk about *your* ex and to assess your Ex Factor. Did you just break up? Has it been a few days, weeks, months? Are you and your ex still speaking? And more importantly, are you still sleeping together? Your answers to these questions are very important because they help us figure out where you are in the breakup timeline. According to the breakup timeline, the more time and distance you put between yourself and your ex, the better your chances are of healing your heart and moving on. Which is why the following rule is crucial to your recovery:

Breakup Rule #1

You cannot sleep with your ex. Some of you may think this is a ridiculous rule. You may be so hurt, angry, or just plain *over* the relationship that you can't possibly imagine sleeping with your ex. But as someone who's been there,

I know just how tempting it is to fall back into the arms of your ex. There's momentary comfort there. Sex with your ex offers that false sense of security that everything's the way it once was. But it's not, which is why you have to follow Breakup Rule #1. It's the first rule I share with you because it's crucial to your recovery. And I think it's worth repeating:

You cannot move on from your Big Breakup while still sleeping with your ex. Just don't do it!

Which leads me to the second rule of breakup recovery.

Breakup Rule #2

Not only can you not sleep with your ex after a breakup, but you should avoid any contact with him at all, including calling, texting, e-mailing, checking his MySpace page, instant messaging, driving by his house, showing up at his work, or leaving notes on his car. (Repeat after me—you cannot move on if you're still holding on!)

FROM THE breakup chronicles

" My ex broke up with me six months ago. Since then we've been carrying on a sexual relationship. Even though we're having sex, I've been trying to move on and date other guys. The problem is, I get confused. Sometimes I think I still have feelings for my ex and sometimes I'm just not sure. *Help!*"

—Candace

I'm going to give you the same advice I gave Candace. *If you're still sleeping with your ex* (or maintaining any kind of contact with him), I want you to find the closest mirror, look into it, and ask yourself why. And then wait for a good answer. Maybe you're holding out hope that the relationship isn't really over. Maybe you're seeking comfort in the arms of someone you love. Or maybe, if you did the dumping, you're trying to soften the blow of the breakup for your ex. (If so, stop it right now.) The harsh reality is that by sleeping with your ex or maintaining any kind of close connection with him immediately following the breakup, you're only delaying your own happiness and making moving on impossible.

And what if you're *not* sleeping with your ex? Look in the mirror and congratulate yourself on how well you're handling your breakup. You are a total breakup recovery rock star!

EX ETIQUETTE

The most common question people ask me on my Web site is whether or not it's possible to stay friends with their ex after a breakup while still moving on. And nine times out of ten my answer is always the same—*no*. Why? Because as hard as it may be to accept, your relationship is over. This person is now your ex. The relationship ended for a reason. It's now time to *ex*tract your ex from your life, give yourself time to heal, and create the space to move on. Most people who try to stay friends with their ex are just doing so in hopes of either rekindling the relationship or using the other person as a crutch until someone better comes along. What happens when it's the other person who moves on first? Ouch!

Of course, there are circumstances in which you can't avoid maintaining a relationship with your ex, and I'll get into that later. But for now, the following is a cheat sheet on appropriate ways of communicating after the Big Breakup.

By Phone

The reasons for talking to your ex on the phone are—wait. There are none. Delete his number from your cell phone.

And if he leaves you a message, listen to it only once in case your million-dollar check from Publishers Clearing House somehow ended up at his address. Then delete immediately and move on. Which brings me to the next breakup rule:

Breakup Rule #3

Do not save phone messages from your ex and replay them over and over just to hear his voice. That's self-destructive and will only hurt your ability to let go and move on. Not sure you're ready, willing, and/or able to move on just yet? Maybe the next breakup secret will help change your mind.

breakup secret #2

There are plenty of available men who would love to call you. It's up to you to clear the way for them, and that means letting go of your ex, giving yourself time to heal, and then making space for someone new in your life.

Via E-mail, IM, Text Messaging, MySpace

After you've arranged to return each other's stuff, delete your ex from your e-mail address book, your MySpace friends list, and your instant messaging contacts. That way when you're having a fragile moment, you're not tempted to contact him. (The repercussions the following day can be embarrassing and costly to your recovery.) And if you were hoping to keep tabs on your ex by tracking his every online move or possible new dating adventures via his MySpace page? Don't. It'll just make you wonder who he's talking to (or obsess about those girls who keep posting messages to him), and you don't need that. Remove his page from your favorites and look for a new friend or two to take his MySpace place.

In Person

Because there are just too many emotions swirling around in your post-breakup head, you should avoid seeing your ex in person at all costs. If you see your ex too soon, you run the risk of suffering potentially bad consequences, including any or all of the following:

1. Losing face by crying hysterically.
2. Waking up beside him the next morning and realizing you just had sex with your ex.
3. Getting arrested for assault and battery.

Let's face it: None of these situations is ideal. So if you can, avoid seeing your ex until your emotions are more stable. Only you can determine when that will be (and it's okay to say *never*!).

When You Can't Cut Your Ex Out of Your Life

If you have to see your ex—if you work together, have children together, if you own property or a business together— you're going to have to work extra hard to successfully move on with your life. It's not impossible; it's just that it's more challenging. But don't worry, you can do it!

Here are some ground rules to follow if you *have to* maintain a relationship with your ex:

1. Create a new set of boundaries (and don't let Mr. Ex cross them).
2. Limit your discussions to only those topics you absolutely have to share, like child-care arrangements or business decisions. *Do not* discuss what you did over

the weekend, if you're dating anyone, or if you'd like to go have coffee sometime.

3. Be firm with your ex (ya gotta be strong!).

4. Always remember that you deserve better (and someone better suited for you *is* out there).

FROM THE **breakup chronicles**

"My ex just won't leave me alone. We broke up over a year ago (he was unfaithful) but he's still in my life because we have two young children together. The problem is, any time I start dating someone, my ex gets territorial and scares the guy off. I just want to move on from this relationship and I'm ready to find someone wonderful, but I'm afraid my ex will ruin any new relationship I might start."

—*Robin*

The most courageous women I've heard from on my Web site and message board are those who have children with an ex who either does not want them to move on or who has already moved on without them. Many of these women are single mothers who hold down two jobs while going to school, and they're just trying to better their lives. If you are one of these fabulous females, stay strong. You're doing everything right. It will get easier. Just give it time and keep those boundaries firmly intact.

House Rules

If at the time of your breakup you and your ex were living together, your post-breakup progress depends upon your ability to clean house. And by that I mean the quicker you part domestic ways, the better. If you can move out? Great!

Sure it can be a costly pain in the butt initially, but it will save your heart a lot of hurt in the long run. By breaking up with both your relationship *and* your shared space, you get to create a whole new home to heal and move on in. (Now *that's* a win-win!)

Moving Out (and On)

If you're the one moving out, do so as quickly as possible. Even if you have to move in with friends momentarily, it's better than crashing at the scene of the crime for weeks on end. You can always put your stuff in storage until you find a more permanent place to live. Or maybe you'll luck out and find the apartment of your dreams in your ideal price range right away. After a particularly painful breakup of mine, I stumbled upon my first solo apartment—a cute studio in my favorite neighborhood within weeks of moving out. I'd initially thought I might be staying at my sister's place for a few months until I found something. (Thanks for the crash pad, Sissy!)

Exit Etiquette

If you're the one who's moving out, arrange a time for you to pack up your belongings when your ex is not home. The less contact you have right now, the better. (You don't want a bad breakup to escalate into a shouting match, restraining orders for the both of you, or worse, a reconciliation with the wrong person!) If at all possible, *do not* rely on your ex to pack your things. As hard as it may be to return to your shared space, you need to be responsible for your stuff. Plus, depending on how your ex feels about the breakup, your belongings might not make it to their new home in one piece.

After you've packed everything up, try to schedule your move for a time when your ex isn't around, too. That will alleviate any unnecessary tension and stress. However, if your ex decides to be difficult, insisting he be there to ensure you're not trashing the apartment in his absence or packing up any of his stuff (like you want his back issues of *FHM* or his video games that used to make you crazy), ask a friend along for moral support. Your ex is less likely to be a jerk if there's a witness.

Staying Put (and Still Moving On!)

And if your ex is the one to heave ho? Show him the same courtesy you'd expect of him by making yourself scarce when he's packing his things and moving out. If you're worried about him trashing or stealing *your* stuff, ask a trustworthy guy friend to supervise in your absence. And try to resolve any security deposit issues, rent worries, or other financial issues amicably (and ASAP). Neither one of you needs to drag things out, act petty, or throw a tantrum. Things are difficult enough right now. You're both adults. Act like it. (And be sure to get his keys back so that you don't have to worry about any post-breakup revenge rage at 3 A.M.)

Exorcising Your Ex

Once your ex has moved out, you'll want to follow these post-breakup rituals to help exorcise your ex:

1. **Get rid of any evidence that your ex actually existed:** This includes old photos, his cologne under your bathroom sink, the alma mater mug he used to slurp coffee from, and so on.
2. **Purchase a bundle of sage and cleanse your space:** You can find sage at New Age shops and health food stores. When in doubt, ask the sales clerk about the best way to smudge your space, or go online and do your own research using the keyword *smudging*. It's pretty easy and no, it doesn't require a degree in the dark arts.
3. **Rearrange furniture so things don't look exactly the same:** Just be sure to plug in a night light so you don't trip over that footstool or bookcase on your 4 A.M. trip to the bathroom.
4. **Replace items your ex took with things that make you happy:** Brighten your space with colorful flowers, a new picture on the wall, or that end table you've been eyeing that your ex always thought was too girly but you're now free to buy.
5. **Sleep in the middle of the bed:** Go ahead, it's *all* yours, Baby!

If you follow these house rules, your breakup recovery will be that much smoother. Of course, there will still be times when it's hard. Just remember—when you're in the middle of all that breakup angst, you're not having a breakdown. You're breaking *up* so that you can eventually move on. (And that totally rocks!)

What to Say If Your Ex Calls, E-mails, or Stops By

After you've parted ways, your ex may decide to be a clueless cad who tries to keep in touch with you. But don't be fooled. It's not a sign from the universe that the two of you should reconcile. And fortunately for you, there's a post-breakup contingency plan for every occasion.

The following are some tips for handling unsolicited contact with your ex.

If He Calls

1. Hang up.
2. Pretend you don't speak English.
3. Say something dirty and then apologize, claiming you thought he was your new boyfriend, a sexy beefcake who eats ex-boyfriends for lunch.
4. Ask to be put on his "Do Not Call" list.
5. Tell him you were actually just thinking about him—that is, imagining him tied naked to a bull's-eye target while you fling razor-sharp knives at him. (That oughtta buy him a clue about not calling you ever again!)

If He E-mails

1. Delete immediately (don't even read it, no matter how tempted you are!).
2. Mark his e-mail address as spam to be filtered by your computer.
3. Block his e-mail address so you can never get e-mail from him again.
4. Forward the e-mail he sent to you to all of your friends with a brief note about how well you're doing and how happy you are since you're no longer with

what's-his-name (oh, and be sure to accidentally BCC your ex!).

5. Google *e-mail virus* and if possible, send him one.

If He Stops By

1. Slam the door in his face.
2. Politely but firmly ask him to leave you alone.
3. Put a serious look on your face, squeeze his arm gently, and tell him that it's time he knew the truth—size *does* matter. (He'll quickly get a clue!)
4. What do you think pepper spray is for?
5. Repeat step 4, followed by step 1.

breakup secret #3

Even though he's still sleeping with you, Mr. Ex is probably moving on.

The Post-Breakup Birds and Bees

Still thinking about maintaining a friendship with your ex while trying to move on? Or are you toying with the idea of getting back into bed with your ex? If you answered yes (or even *maybe*) to either of those questions, I've got another question for you. What's going to happen when one of you starts dating someone else? It *will* happen—and you may not be the first to move on. As someone who stumbled upon a photo of the new girl long before I'd moved on, I now know that I never should have let Mr. Ex back into my bed after the Big Breakup. Every time we slept together, it opened up the possibility in my mind that we might get back together again (even though I did the dumping—twice!). It took the pain of seeing the new girl's photo to finally snap me out of my delusion.

It wasn't pretty, but it was the kick in the pants that I needed to make me walk away for good.

FROM THE **breakup chronicles**

❝My ex and I broke up a little over a month ago. When we were together, he didn't treat me like he should have and I know I deserve better. I also know in my heart that I really don't want to be with him but sometimes I get sad that I couldn't make the relationship work. And then I get lonely thinking about him and looking at all my friends who are all in great relationships. I start to wonder what's wrong with me. And that's when I pick up the phone and call him, even though I know I shouldn't.❞

—*Kristina*

What's it gonna take for you to move on?

Breakups Are Like Band-Aids

Walking away after a breakup can be one of the hardest things you ever do. Especially when you mistake the intensity of your feelings following a breakup with the distorted notion that your mixed emotions mean Mr. Ex must have been The One. If he had been The One, the relationship would not have ended. Having said that, it's just better to peel your breakup off quickly, feel the pain, and be done with it. By sticking around after the breakup, all you're really doing is prolonging the inevitable and not allowing yourself to move on. And you deserve to move on and be happy!

Look at it this way. Now that your ex is no longer in the picture, you're free to be your amazing self, live your life, and eventually meet someone new. Someone better suited for you. Maybe even The One (if that's what you're looking for). Isn't that worth a little heartache along the way?

Proof Positive

Still looking for signs that you are *not* a failure at love? Look around. Those married and/or coupled up friends you envy? They're only one successful relationship ahead of you. Before their current relationship, they went through their fair share of breakups. They got their hearts broken by Mr. or Ms. Wrong, too. At times they most likely felt like failures at love, too. Repeat after me: You are *not* a loser at love. By breaking up with the wrong person, you have poised yourself for future relationship success with someone who's right for you!

breakup secret #4
The sooner you let go of your ex, the sooner you'll move on. (What have you got to lose?)

between-chapter *check-in*

Before we move on to the next chapter, let's briefly check in. How are you feeling? This breakup stuff can be tricky, so it's important to be nice to yourself and to be patient with your recovery. In the spaces to the right, or in your breakup recovery journal, I want you to write down five adjectives that describe your current emotional state. This is an exercise we'll repeat between chapters throughout Part One to chart your progress. Keep in mind there are no right or wrong answers. So go ahead, record your five emotions. (It's perfectly okay to have positive feelings about the breakup, too!)

Need help? Feel free to borrow from the emotions listed on the facing page.

DATE

_____

_____

_____

_____

_____

ANGRY confused

betrayed HURT

sad *embarrassed*

vulnerable devastated

relieved grateful

BITTER mortified

exhausted numb

furious depressed

manic AFRAID

lost overwhelmed

free PEACEFUL

CHAPTER TWO
the slump
aka "woe is me"

So far I've been talking a lot about how to distance yourself from your ex. I think it's important to set up some ground rules for your new life right away. But now that we're clear about ex etiquette, we can move on to more important topics like dealing with the fact that you just went through your Big Breakup and you're probably feeling a lot of strong emotions. And that's good! It means you're dealing with your breakup in a healthy way.

The spectrum of emotions you're feeling right now may depend on how the Big Breakup went down. As I said before, there are many different kinds of Big Breakups. Some happen suddenly, out of the blue like an avalanche. Others begin as a low rumble, increasing in volume and strength as time goes on until the earth splits open and so does the relationship. And others snap like a tree branch during a tornado.

If you think comparing breakups to natural disasters is a little odd, bear with me. The truth is both are forces of nature—powerful, unpredictable, and often destructive. Both can sweep us off our feet, send us running for cover, and obliterate our lives as we know them. And when both phenomena subside, it's sometimes hard to put our lives back together.

What kind of natural disaster best describes your breakup?

The Earthquake Breakup

When you think about your Big Breakup, could you feel the end coming long before it actually arrived? Were there little tremors along the way that you may have chosen to ignore—seismic activity like increased arguments, major misunderstandings, and deepening drama? Were you or your partner expressing feelings of dissatisfaction months ago, only to let it remain unresolved until one day you had a huge fight and suddenly your relationship was over?

HERE'S HOW THE EARTHQUAKE BREAKUP CAN FEEL

"Like you're on an emotional roller coaster and you just can't control which feeling comes next. One minute I'm crying, the next minute I'm pissed off. And the next? Who knows?**"**

—Sacha

If so, then your Big Breakup was like an earthquake measuring 7.0 on the Richter scale. If you still feel like the ground is shaking, that's understandable. You may also be feeling these things:

Resentful
Depressed
Fragile
Overwhelmed

The Avalanche

Did your Big Breakup come as a bit of a shock to you? Did everything in your relationship seem to be going along just fine and then out of the blue—*bam!*—it was over? Were you the dumpee, left standing there with that dumbfounded look on your face long after your ex delivered the one-two punch, also known as *It's over?*

HERE'S HOW THE AVALANCHE BREAKUP CAN FEEL

"Numb. Like I can't function. Like I'm walking through life as usual, only nothing's the same and I can't do anything about it.**"**

—*Melanie*

Still shaking your head and wondering *Why?* Chances are your breakup was like an avalanche. It's no wonder you sometimes feel like you can't breathe. You've just been emotionally buried! In the case of an avalanche breakup, you may also be feeling these things:

Betrayed
Irrational
Devastated
Angry

The Tornado

Like that tree branch that suddenly snapped during the tornado, your Big Breakup may have felt like a snap decision. But underneath it all, signs of weakness had been building for some time. Your sex life might have been suffering. Maybe you weren't communicating as well or as easily as you once did. Maybe job stress or changes/disagreements about personal priorities (including decisions about marriage, children, and home buying) were causing relationship clashes and increased friction between the two of you.

HERE'S HOW THE TORNADO BREAKUP CAN FEEL

"Like someone just reached into my body, pulled out some unnamed organ, and left a huge gaping hole that now feels incredibly empty.**"**

—*Maria*

Many mutual Big Breakups—that is, when both of you agree to call it quits—fit into the tornado scenario. And while you may have partially initiated the end of your relationship, you probably still feel some of this:

Confused
Sad
Anxious
Exhausted

The Emotional Roller Coaster

Interspersed between all of these difficult emotions, you may also be feeling a little bit relieved. There may even be moments when you feel manic elation about your sudden freedom from a relationship that just wasn't working anymore. You may be prone to fits of laughter followed by a torrent of tears. Moments later, you might experience strong surges of panic, isolation, loneliness, and despair. Don't worry—you're not crazy. You're just post-breakup. And like the old song says, breaking up *is* hard to do. You're entitled to feel blue (not to mention red hot, dull gray, and fiery orange) while going through your Big Breakup. In fact, you're allowed to wallow in any and/or all of your intense feelings. It's called the Post-Breakup Slump. And before you can really and truly move on from your breakup, you must first celebrate your slump.

....

Post-Breakup To-Do List

Cry

Cry a lot

Cry some more

Repeat as needed

Exactly how do you celebrate a slump? Everyone's technique is probably a little different. What follows are some tried-and-true ways to celebrate your slump and the do's and don'ts of each method.

The Solitary Slump, aka Spend the Entire Weekend at Home Alone

After your Big Breakup, you may feel the need to spend some quality time wallowing by yourself. So clear your social calendar, stock up on supplies, and settle in for the ultimate weekend of wallowing. It's time to embrace your inner hermit and dive headfirst into your slump!

....

Solitary Slump Tips

Do Wear your favorite pajamas 24/7, watch lots of bad TV, cry your eyes out.

Don't Shower, answer the phone, brush your hair *or* your teeth.

Weekend of wallow checklist Comfort food (ice cream, mashed potatoes, chocolate, and other sweets or salty snacks); comfy clothes (pajamas, sweats, old T-shirts); several boxes of tissues; appropriate music and/

or DVDs; a journal (it helps to get all those icky feelings out on paper!).

Recommended music Alanis Morrisette, Rachel Yamagata, Indigo Girls, Tina Turner, Aimee Mann (Girl Power all the way!).

Recommended DVDs *Addicted to Love* (great revenge flick!), *Thelma & Louise* (female bonding plus male bashing at its finest), *Me Myself I* starring Rachel Griffiths (must-see Girl Power movie!), and *Sex & the City* seasons one through six (featuring the break-ups and makeups of Carrie, Samantha, Miranda, and Charlotte).

The Shopping Slump, aka Retail Therapy

After your breakup, you may find that everything reminds you of your ex, *including* your wardrobe. If this is the case, then a girl's gotta do what a girl's gotta do—go shopping! Now, because there's a lot of prep time involved in this particular slump celebration, you'll want to clear your *entire* schedule and make way for some serious post-breakup pampering. You may even need to take a mental health day off from work. (Seriously!)

COMFORT FOOD HALL PASS

Okay, you're going through a breakup. That's earned you a temporary comfort-food hall pass, which means you're now free to engage in a little emotional eating. Stock your pantry and freezer with your fave foods, whatever they may be. And don't beat yourself up for overindulging. This is one of the few times in life when it's perfectly acceptable to wear stretchy pants and have a dinner menu consisting of nothing but carbs. Don't worry about it. You'll put the pudding down when you're ready. In the meantime, enjoy!

Once you've cleared your calendar, the first order of business is a mani-pedi (and any waxing that you might need done), followed by a trip to your favorite lingerie store (a girl can't spend all that time in a dressing room after a breakup without having the cutest bra-and-panty set that *doesn't* remind her of her ex!). Then a decadent lunch at your favorite restaurant will help you power up for an afternoon of retail therapy. Don't even think about skipping dessert—you'll burn the extra calories off during your shopping spree. (Plus, remember, your breakup has just earned you a comfort-food hall pass.) And should your retail romp go into overtime, be sure to have a protein bar in your purse. But don't lose too much track of time because the best is yet to come. An end-of-day massage will work out those knots you got lugging around your new loot. Then later that night or the very next day, put on a fabulous fashion show for your friends. You're sure to forget all about your ex in no time. (Work it, girl!)

Shopping Slump Tips

Do Buy something your ex would have hated, bring along a shopping buddy, splurge a little.

Don't Max out your credit cards, buy anything that will remind you of your ex (if he loved you in red, buy something purple), shop somewhere that you might run into your ex (too close to the breakup for a face-to-face encounter).

Retail therapy checklist Credit card and/or cash, dark sunglasses, a shopping buddy, comfy shoes that are easy to slip on and off (and show off your pretty painted toes!).

The Escapist Slump, aka Girls' Weekend

If you lived with your ex, you'll most likely want to get out of the house (or crime scene—you decide), and find a whole new scene to wallow in. Chances are you won't want to do it alone, which is where your Boo-Hoo Crew comes in.

Your what? Your Boo-Hoo Crew, also known as your new best friends. I'll talk about them later in the chapter, but for now, keep in mind that your Boo-Hoo Crew is essential to your recovery. They're the ones who will cheer you up, remind you of your Fabulous Factor when you forget, and get you through your post-breakup slump.

· ·

Escapist Slump Tips

Do Let your g.f.'s take care of you, go someplace that doesn't remind you of your ex, allow yourself to get a little tipsy (just be sure you have a designated driver).

Don't Revisit a location you went to with your ex or go somewhere that you and your ex were planning on going, and *most especially* do not get so hammered that you end up locked in your hotel bathroom, drunk-dialing your ex on your cell phone.

Possible locations include A spa retreat, a rustic but thoroughly modern cabin in the mountains (complete with cable TV, DVD player, indoor plumbing, and a fully equipped kitchen, of course); Las Vegas (not suitable for every gal going through her Big Breakup, but if you can pull off sipping margaritas poolside while sniffling behind sunglasses, then go for it!).

Suggested activities Massage, mani-pedi, happy hour, a long nap, ex-boyfriend bonfire (what are fireplaces for?!).

The Fetal Position Slump, aka A Visit to Mom and Dad

And then there are times after a breakup when you just want to be pampered. A trip to see Mom and Dad may be just what the doctor ordered. Keep in mind that not everyone's parents are equipped to handle the Big Breakup. Only you'll know if that trip to see them will be therapeutic or something to send you into therapy. Use your best judgment.

FROM THE **breakup chronicles**

"After my last breakup, I couldn't eat or sleep for days. I stayed in bed and cried all weekend for weeks on end. It just hurt so bad. But eventually it did get better. I ended up losing fifteen pounds because of the breakup. And once I stopped spending my weekends in bed, I decided to keep the pounds off by eating right and exercising regularly. I lost ten more pounds, got a new 'do, and splurged on a new wardrobe. Thanks to the breakup, my life and my body changed dramatically for the better!**"**

—Nikki

If Mom's homemade chocolate chip cookies are the comfort food you seek, or Dad's homespun advice and support have helped you through other tough times, then head on home for some old-fashioned recuperation. However, if their constant questions about what went wrong *this time* are going to bring you down, just don't do it!

Fetal Position Slump Tips

Do Take long bubble baths, eat your favorite comfort foods, curl up in your childhood blanket or family quilt, and enjoy some good old-fashioned TLC.

Don't Divulge too much (some parents want to judge or fix everything), cry too much (this just freaks Mom and Dad out), stay too long (there's a reason you left home, after all!).

The Scary Slump, aka Embrace Your Anger

Some consider this risky post-breakup behavior, but I don't think you can really move on from a badly broken heart without first moving through your anger. So if you feel the need to spew, then this is the slump for you! While I don't recommend stewing for days, weeks, months on end, I do encourage getting in touch with your rage (in small doses, of course!). And remember, these intense emotions *will* subside—just give them time.

Scary Slump Tips

Do Invest in a harmless voodoo doll, make use of your aggression by signing up for a kickboxing or martial arts class, improve your aim by practicing archery or darts (you never know when this will come in handy), go hog wild on the bumper cars at your local amusement park (just be sure to steer clear of children without helmets during your scary slump!).

Don't Call or e-mail your ex while in a venomous state, do anything that could get you arrested (like bash your ex's car windows in), spend too much time obsessing about *what went wrong.*

Suggested activities Destroy all evidence of your ex (burn pictures, shred birthday cards and other love notes); kickbox your way through your rage; yell, scream, and/or curse your ex for as long as it takes for you to feel better.

(And if those thoughts of revenge and/or getting even still keep you up at night? Set those feelings aside. We'll deal with them in Chapter 3.)

The Pity Party Slump, aka The Major Boo-Hoo Blues

Because there are times when you just can't let go of your ex until you've seriously mourned him, the Boo-Hoo Blues are a must. Of course, this type of slump celebration requires serious drama-queen behavior, including bawling your eyes out while wearing his old sweatshirt, slobbering over old pictures of the two of you together, and looking up at the ceiling and screaming *Why?* over and over again.

A word of caution: The Boo-Hoo Blues are not for the faint of heart. You've gotta be willing to *really* wallow in your pain and misery, which can be tricky post-Big Breakup behavior and may require an intervention from your Boo-Hoo Crew (see the next section). And because this method is questionable, the only do's and don'ts are these: Do this in the privacy of your own home, and *do not* contact your ex under any circumstances during the Major Boo-Hoo Blues. (Ya gotta stay strong!)

So there you have it—time-tested tools for celebrating your slump. Feel free to pick and choose the methods that work for you. When in doubt, refer to the cheat sheet that follows.

Post-Breakup Slump Do's and Don'ts

Do:

○ Reach out to friends who are supportive and nurturing.
○ Keep a journal of your feelings.
○ Engage in pampering behavior like taking bubble baths, snuggling up with a good book in bed, getting a thera-peutic massage.

Don't:
○ Obsess about your feelings.
○ Reach out to your ex in a moment of weakness.
○ Engage in dangerous behavior like driving under the influence, having reckless (and unprotected) rebound sex, or inflicting bodily harm upon yourself (not to mention drunk dialing!).

Assembling Your Boo-Hoo Crew

In order to get you through your Big Breakup and the resulting slump, you're going to need to assemble a crack team of fabulous female friends. Part cheerleader, part therapist, your Boo-Hoo Crew should be reliable, patient, and consist of at least three girlfriends for round-the-clock supervision and support.

The role of the Boo-Hoo Crew is to provide the following:

○ A shoulder to cry on
○ A voice of reason
○ Damage control (in case you get the urge to contact your ex)
○ The bright side

Tips for Assembling the Perfect Boo-Hoo Crew

Not everyone's cut out to be a Boo-Hoo Crew member. It's important to recruit only those friends who are up to the challenge. While assembling your crew, keep the following considerations in mind:

○ Include only girlfriends who are loving and supportive.
○ Exclude any so-called g.f.'s who might say things like "I told you so," brag about their own relationship, or ask

if they can call your ex (in fact, dump these "friends" immediately!).

○ *Do not* include any mutual friends who might report back to your ex on your progress (and/or dish about your setbacks).

The Boo-Hoo Crew Code of Honor

During your slump, your Boo-Hoo Crew should be available 24/7. It may sound like a tremendous commitment, but that's what friends are for. You'd do it for them (if you haven't already). And let's face it: There are times in life when you have to sleep in shifts. This just happens to be one of those times.

There are also going to be times when you'll obsess about your ex, times when you'll want your ex back, and times when all you can think about is picking up the phone and calling your ex. These are the times when you should rely on your Boo-Hoo Crew for support. You'll want to choose g.f.'s who know you well enough to know when you need comfort versus when you need a kick in the pants. Friends who can remind you of the nitpicky negative things you once said about your ex that you're going to forget when you're wishing you two were still together. Your Boo-Hoo Crew should always know (and be able to remind you) why your ex wasn't good for you then, and why he's definitely not worth pining over now.

Why Your Ex Isn't Worth Pining Over

○ He's not right for you.
○ Someone else is out there, and you're free to look for him.
○ You deserve to feel loved and wanted (and super sexy).
○ He's probably not pining over you (harsh, but probably true).

When we're in post-breakup mode, some of us have trouble reaching out to others. We think asking for help is a sign of weakness, but it's not. It's a show of strength. So go out there and recruit the best Boo-Hoo Crew ever! (Right now.)

Post-Breakup Behavior to Avoid

We've all been there. We've all done it. And it's one of the most dangerous things you can do during your post-breakup slump. What is it?

Putting your ex on a pedestal. While we know he wasn't perfect when we were with him, we sometimes forget that he's not going to suddenly become perfect without us. After a breakup, we somehow think that all of Mr. Ex's imperfections either have or will someday soon miraculously disappear. We convince ourselves that now that he's no longer with us, he's become that amazing individual we always wished he could be.

FROM THE **breakup chronicles**

❝ After my breakup, I realized I had made my boyfriend such a central part of what my existence meant that the world seemed dark and pointless when we broke up. What was the point of living if he and his love were the only things that I found completed me? I had to figure out a way to stop focusing on my ex and learn to love myself. It wasn't easy, but I did it. And my life is so much richer now. **❞**

—*Amanda*

After my Big Breakup, I somehow convinced myself that all of my ex's flaws had vanished. And yes, to his credit, he did a lot of self-reflection and self-improvement after the breakup—he started volunteering, spent less time with his controlling father, cleaned up his finances with the help of an inheritance. But ultimately that didn't change who he was or why I really broke up with him. He was still moody. He still resented my independence. He still didn't quite "get" me. If we had stayed together, he still would have been secretive and hid things from me. At the end of the day he still wasn't the right guy for me. I owed it to myself to keep searching for that right guy and not settle for less than I deserved. (And you do, too!)

breakup secret #5

Nobody's perfect, *including* and most especially your ex. So avoid the pedestal. It'll not only make your post-breakup recovery a whole lot easier, but moving on will be easier, too!

Erase "If Only" from Your Vocabulary

After a breakup, especially the Big Breakup, we're prone to self-defeating thoughts and low self-esteem. For some reason, our gender is just wired that way. It's only natural for us to look back on our relationship and wonder if there's anything we could have done differently.

But here's a newsflash that may change how you feel— your ex is most likely not looking back and wondering if he could have done anything differently to salvage the relationship. He's probably not beating himself up over the breakup. So why should you? What's done is done, and it's for the best. You may not know that today, but you will know it very soon. In an effort to get there as quickly as possible, it's important to erase *if only* from your vocabulary. So right here and now, let's take a moment to erase the following sentences:

If only I'd done _____ .
(As in, "If only I'd done more to make it work.")

If only I'd said _____ .
(As in, "If only I'd said I was sorry and kept trying.")

If only I wasn't _____ .
(As in, "If only I wasn't so confused/needy/etc.")

If only he'd _____ .
(As in, "If only he'd love me more/get his act together.")

The truth is that you did everything in your power to make your relationship work. In fact, you probably worked overtime to fix the problems, even if they weren't your problems to begin with. And things still didn't work out. That doesn't mean you failed. It just means that this particular relationship wasn't meant to be. (It also means there's someone else out there who's a better partner for you, and you're now available to find him!) Second-guessing yourself with all those *if only*'s will *only* torture you. So, like his phone number and e-mail address, delete *if only* from your memory.

The Dangers of "Why?"

Another word to strike from your post-breakup vocabulary: *Why?* You'll never get a satisfactory answer. And asking it will inevitably drive you nuts, not to mention slow down your recovery. So stop asking the question. (Right now.)

Rules of the Blame Game

Toward the end of your relationship, were you and your ex playing the Blame Game? You know how it is; everything is either your fault or his fault. And once the breakup actually happens, the Blame Game gets more competitive. You tell all your friends what he did, and he tells all his friends what you did. You're hoping everyone takes your side (of course so is he).

Stop for a minute. Think about what you're doing. What are you getting out of playing this silly game? Sympathy? Maybe. But wouldn't you rather be the one who walked away and moved on without playing petty games? Don't you think your friends would be more impressed if you didn't spread your breakup b.s. around? (The answer is *Yes*.)

RECOVERY ℞

Need a little lift? Send yourself some balloons or flowers at work but don't include a card. Let people wonder who they're from. Whenever you're having a moody moment, look at the balloons or flowers and remember just how amazing you really are (and how brave you are to be going through your Big Breakup and *still* showing up for work every day!).

The truth is that your real friends don't care whose fault it is. They only care about your well-being. And they'd much rather help you move on from this breakup than watch you wallow and obsess about what went wrong and who's to blame. (As for how to handle your relationship with mutual friends after the breakup, I'll discuss that in Chapter 3.)

And now back to the Blame Game.

When it comes to the Blame Game, I have only one rule. Don't play it. Maybe he cheated. Maybe he lied. Maybe he was just a big jerk. (Or maybe you cheated, lied, or acted like a big jerk.) But what's the point of pointing the finger, other than to stall your own progress in moving on? What's done is done. So for now, keep your participation in the Blame Game to a minimum.

An Ex-orcism Exercise

Now that the breakup fog is starting to lift, take another look around your space. Are there remnants of Mr. Ex lingering? Chances are, you haven't completely extracted your ex from your environment. And that's okay. But now's the time to clear any remaining clutter. That magnet on the fridge with the cutesy saying that reminds you of him? Get rid of it! His two-in-one shampoo that's still in the shower? Toss it! The boxer shorts you come across next time you do laundry? Not a sentimental memento that deserves any tears. Just ditch 'em! You'll be so much better off once you've completely exorcised your ex's stuff. I know it's hard, but it's for the best. So get rid of any ex-related items that are still hanging around. (Right now.) And then congratulate yourself for being such a breakup recovery rock star!

Regardless of how it happened, it's happened—your Big Breakup. By now, the reality (and enormity) of the situation has probably sunk in, along with the realization that certain things will never be the same, such as your heart, for one. At this point, I once again congratulate you on your breakup! And I remind you that out of all this pain, something amazing will come. Maybe not today. Maybe not next week. But one day soon enough, you will be giving thanks for your Big Breakup. (In the meantime, feel free to get down and dirty with your slump.)

between-chapter *check-in*

Before we move on to Chapter 3, let's do a brief check-in. How are you feeling? Strong, healthy, empowered? If so, fantastic! Your breakup recovery is progressing nicely. If you're still feeling like a puffy-eyed blubbering mess, don't worry. You're doing just fine. Right now you're in the middle of your slump. It's important to celebrate and wallow in it. The slump can be comfortable. And for the time being, that's okay. But guess what? There will come a time when the slump is the last place you'll want to be. When your slump will feel worse than letting go of your ex. The day will come when you'll *want* to dump your slump and move on. And that's the place I want you to get to. That's the place we'll get to together.

DATE

In the meantime, write down your five emotions here or in your journal. There are no right or wrong answers. Just identify how you're feeling right now. (You might even be annoyed with having to write down your feelings. Feel free to write about that!)

Compare this list with your previous list on page 26. What's changed? What's stayed the same? Your answers may pinpoint where you're struggling in your post-breakup recovery. Or they may reflect just how well you're doing. Pay attention to recurring thoughts, feelings, or issues that surface in the coming weeks.

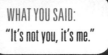

WHAT YOU SAID:
"It's not you, it's me."

WHAT YOU MEANT:
"It's so you."

CHAPTER THREE
rebounding, revenge,
and other post-breakUP rules

Once upon a time, conventional breakup wisdom went something like this:

the only way to get over a man is with *a new man*

And while this breakup philosophy may have been followed by some of our favorite famous Jens (Lopez and Garner) during their single days, I don't recommend adopting it for yourself. It's *so* last millennium. In fact, in the twenty-first century, there's a much healthier post-breakup philosophy, and it goes something like this:

the only way to get over a breakup is to *get through it* and move on

To avoid relationship rebounding during your own recovery, take a look at the questionable rebounding of these famous Jens:

· ·

Famous Relationship Rebounders

Jennifer Lopez Hubby #1 Ojani Noa ➜ P Diddy (or Daddy or Puffy) ➜ Hubby #2 Cris Judd ➜ Fiancé Ben Affleck ➜ Hubby #3 Marc Anthony

Jennifer Garner Hubby #1 and *Felicity* costar Scott Foley ➜ *Alias* costar Michael Vartan ➜ *Daredevil* costar (and Hubby #2) Ben Affleck

Not only are the famous Jens impressive rebounders, but how 'bout that Ben? From Gwyn(eth) to Jen #1 to Jen #2. Hopefully, he—along with those famous Jens—has learned his breakup lessons from those infamous rebounds and has found *happily ever after* with Ms. Garner. (They do make a cute couple and adorable parents to daughter Violet!)

Think of another famous Jen—Jennifer Aniston. After her Big Breakup, she didn't immediately run into the arms of another man. Neither did Halle Berry. Or Nicole Kidman. These famous females all went through very public Big Breakups and they coped in healthy ways like focusing on their careers, working on themselves, and relying on the comfort of friends (Naomi Watts and Courteney Cox Arquette are definitely Boo-Hoo Crew material!).

If we can learn anything from these heartbreak survivors, it's that nothing is more empowering than handling your Big Breakup with style, class, and self-awareness. Having said that, nobody handles their breakup flawlessly, especially not a Big Breakup. There are going to be times when you'll behave inappropriately (i.e. cry in public, say or do something a bit irrational, show up for work in your pajamas) and we'll just have to chalk that up to PBT (Post-Breakup Trauma). It's okay to be a mess, as long as that messiness is kept to a minimum around people who might get word back to your ex that you're not handling the breakup very well. That's the goal during your slump—to avoid letting your ex think he got the best of you or that you're completely crushed because of him. Don't get me wrong. You can be completely crushed. Just keep your public outbursts and other displays of devastation to a minimum. When you're in the privacy of your own home? Ball your fabulous friggin' eyes out!

Getting to Know Your Breakup

At the moment, you may be on the fence about how you want to handle your Big Breakup. While a part of you wants to handle the breakup with dignity, there may be another part that isn't ready to be the bigger person. Maybe part of you secretly wants revenge. Or maybe you're feeling fragile, and you think that rebounding might be the quick fix you need. Or maybe you want to enlist all your friends in your new post–Big Breakup army and wage an all-out war on your ex until he's friendless (and waving the white surrender flag!).

The quiz on the following page will help determine how you may want to handle your Big Breakup. Once we determine your recovery style, we can address appropriate ways to handle all that broken-hearted anger and/or angst.

Rebounding

Nothing can make a fab female feel more unwanted or unattractive than getting dumped, especially if she thought

Post-Big Breakup Quiz

Which movie title best describes how you feel about your breakup?

1. *Revenge of the Sith*
2. *War of the Roses*
3. *The Big Easy*

The next time you see your ex you'd most like to:

1. Kick him in the crotch.
2. Tell his best friend all the horrible things your ex ever said about him.
3. Be seen making out with a hottie.

You're at a bar with your friends when your ex sends over a cocktail. You:

1. Throw it in his face.
2. Send it back, then buy a round of shots for all your ex's friends (excluding your ex, of course!).
3. Take a sip, then turn to the cute guy on the stool next to you and ask if he wants your cherry.

When you're feeling down about your Big Breakup, who's the first person you call?

1. An acquaintance who happens to work in the parking violations bureau and who also hates your ex.
2. A mutual friend who's sure to take your side.
3. A potential booty call.

Post–Big Breakup Quiz scoring

Scoring: Let's take a look at your answers and see how they affect your approach to your post-breakup recovery. If most of your answers were 1, then chances are you're cooking up revenge fantasies in your spare time. If most of your answers were 2, then you may be looking to recruit *his* friends to your side of the breakup border. And if you mostly chose 3 as your answer, then you may also be considering a Brazilian wax to kick-start your candidacy for Resident Rebounder.

Regardless of how you answered the quiz questions, chances are you're at least *thinking* about some risky post-breakup behavior. That's okay. Nobody's perfect. But before you hop into bed with a stranger or sign up for target practice at the shooting range, I think it's important to address the various post-breakup tactics you may employ and the do's and don'ts of each one.

everything was going along just fine. Meeting someone new, on the other hand, can be exhilarating. It can make you feel beautiful, desirable (and even downright naughty!), which may be exactly what you're seeking post-breakup. And while hooking up with someone new may delay the post-breakup pain you're feeling, it will not mend your broken heart.

Let me say that again. Rebounding after a breakup may be a quick fix, but it will not repair the emotional damage that your breakup caused. It will not erase the memory of your ex. It will not heal your heartbreak. And it will not make you feel better in the long run. Only time can do that. If, however, you decide that a rebound relationship is in your future, the following are a few time-tested tips to help navigate this tricky terrain.

And when rebounding, remember this:

○ Be honest about your intentions with your rebound guy.
○ Jumping into another relationship doesn't mean you're over your ex.
○ Always, always practice safe sex. (Nobody needs a broken heart *and* an STD!)

Honesty Is the Best Policy

When it comes to rebounding, it's important to be honest with everyone involved—that means yourself, your friends, and the object of your rebound affection.

FROM THE **breakup chronicles**

❝ My ex and I were together for three years. He was my first love. After a year and a half of dating, we became pregnant and had a beautiful baby girl. Everything was perfect until my health began to fade. I have arthritis and it got worse after the birth. I ended up in a wheelchair for six months. During this time, my ex broke up with me and moved in with a girl from work. I was devastated. Not only was I in physical pain, I was now in emotional pain. Today I'm happy to report that I'm no longer in a wheelchair and am doing great. And I can easily look back and say *Good riddance!* ❞

—*Jenny*

First, it's important to figure out what you're emotionally equipped to handle at this point. Sometimes harmless flirtation is all you need to feel like your sensational self again. Then again, you may have your mind set on a one-night-stand–style rebound. If this is the case, be sure you know what you're getting into. And be sure to tell at least one member of your Boo-Hoo Crew so that if she can't talk you out of it, she at least knows what (and who) you're doing.

Keep in mind that sex with a stranger won't make the memory of your ex any dimmer. It will most likely just add to your confusion and/or create more internal drama. But because being a fab female also means being pretty stubborn sometimes, a gal's gonna do what a gal's gonna do.

FROM THE breakup chronicles

"After my last breakup, I got wicked drunk and hooked up with some random guy I met at a party. The next morning, I had a massive hangover and loads of regret.**"**

—*Amber*

Here are the do's and don'ts of rebounding:

Do See your rebound for what it is (a temporary quick fix), as well as what it is not (a replacement for your last relationship or a way to heal your heart).

Don't Engage in unprotected sex, or lead anyone on (as in rebounding with a nice guy who's looking for a girlfriend).

Location, Location, Location

If you're serious about seeking out a rebound relationship, the following are some possible places to recruit your rebound guy:

Bars and clubs *Happily ever after* rarely starts on the dance floor at the club or on the bar stool next to you, but a rockin' rebound? Maybe! Just be prepared for cheesy pickup lines and beer breath.

At the gym If you're looking for a muscle man to distract you from your broken heart, sidle up to Bicep Boy and ask him for some workout tips. It'll give his ego a stroke (and possibly he'll return the favor later!).

Online We've all trolled for Mr. Right online, but now's the time to seek out Mr. Right Now. A word of warning: Avoid marriage-minded sites. Look for casual dating sites where you're more likely to meet potential rebound candidates (and not lead anyone looking for a wife astray).

Qualified Candidates

The sexy stranger You're on vacation, he's on vacation. What's a little rebounding between strangers?

Guy passing through town Maybe he's your best guy friend's buddy. Or maybe he's a friend of a friend of a friend. In any event, someone can vouch for him, and that's good enough for you!

The barfly You'd never date him, but that cutie on the bar stool may just rock your world for a night or two!

Not-So-Qualified Candidates

The coworker Rebounding at work is a good idea only if you're planning on changing jobs the very next day.

Your best friend's brother Sure you've always had a crush on him, but rebounding with your best friend's brother is a bad idea (unless of course you're shopping for a new best friend).

The nice guy who's crushing on you He's always looked at you with those longing eyes. And until now, you never thought of him as anything more than a sweet little puppy. Keep it that way. (Translation: Don't mess around with the nice guy when you're rebounding. Breakup karma is a bitch, and it will find you!)

Another ex When trying to get over one ex, it's just not a good idea to sleep with another ex. ('Nuf said!)

The married guy These guys are off-limits, in general, but it's especially important when you're rebounding. Nobody needs that much drama.

The Fabulous Female's Guide to Revenge

Do revenge fantasies keep you up at night? Does the idea of making your ex pay for the pain he's caused you sound enticing? Don't worry—you're not alone. Every red-blooded woman in her right mind has at one time or another premeditated a satisfying revenge plot against her ex. But here's the truth about revenge. The fantasy may be sweet, but the reality can come with jail time. So before you do anything stupid (and possibly end up with a restraining order or a mug shot), think about this. Is your ex really worth any more of your time, energy, or creativity? Clearly, he didn't appreciate those things to begin with. Why should he get any of them now?

THE PERFECT REVENGE PLOT

I Used to Miss Him . . . But My Aim Is Improving, by Alison James

Instead of checking into a jail cell, check out this fun and funny book on post-breakup revenge fantasies! As Alison James says, "The feeling of personal power that comes from dreaming and scheming is liberating, and it helps us get back on our feet. It is not something we should be ashamed of, but instead is a comical sign of how resilient and spunky we truly are."

Rather than waste any more time on an idiot who either let you get away, or did something stupid enough to get dumped by someone as amazing as you, why not refocus all that energy on yourself and your new life? Why not treat yourself to something special, like a day at the spa, or a new cut, color, and highlights, or a weekend cruise to some tropical paradise? I don't know about you, but to me that sounds like time better spent. You deserve to feel beautiful, empowered, and inspired to get on with your life. (And besides, looking and feeling fabulous *is* the best revenge, after all!)

If, however, your breakup has you seeing red—as in revenge—the following are some revenge fantasies followed by revenge realities as well as some suggestions for what to do with all that pent-up rage.

Trash His Reputation

If you're thinking of pulling a Samantha Jones (á la *Sex & the City*) and papering your ex's neighborhood with his photo and a list of the deadly sins he committed, think again. This kind of risky revenge fantasy could land you in the slammer. Not only would you have to worry about a broken heart, you'd have a police record, too.

Instead, why not go online and trash his reputation while maintaining a little anonymity? I'm always looking for scathing, saucy, and/or dishy breakup stories on my Web site, online at *www.breakupchronicles.com*. However, if you want to use your ex's real name to get even, you'll have to look elsewhere. I protect the anonymity of all exes on my site. I just happen to think that writing the story should be therapeutic enough. But fear not, Revenge Seeker. There are plenty of other sites where you can trash your ex's name. Check out Breakupnews.com, WomenSavers.com (formerly ManHaters.com), and DontDateHimGirl.com. You can also create a revenge plot of your very own on one of the many blogging sites out there or on your MySpace page. It's important, however, to keep in mind that one of the possible consequences of your vengeful actions could be that in six months, when you've met someone new and fabulous, your online revenge tactics could chase that new guy far, far away. Is your ex really worth it?

Trash His Stuff

We've all seen plenty of movies and television shows where the jilted girlfriend dumps her ex's stuff out of a two-story window onto the front lawn. Or she burns it all in the fireplace or in an ex-boyfriend bonfire. And yes, that may feel good momentarily. But it may also earn you a Psycho Ex reputation that could follow you into your next relationship. At the end of the day, is that something you really want? Of course you're hurt. Of course you're angry. Of course you want revenge! But why not do something more useful with that red-hot ire? Like, pack up all his remaining stuff and donate it to a homeless shelter. He still loses out on his favorite blue shirt, his overbearing cologne, and his auto-graphed baseball glove. But someone else who really needs it reaps the benefits. (Sounds like a win-win to me! Oh, and be sure to keep the receipt. You can write it off at tax time as a charitable contribution, you do-gooder you!)

Trash Him

If the idea of slashing your ex's tires or mowing him down at the crosswalk or setting fire to his apartment sounds appealing, you might want to stay away from all sharp objects until you're feeling more rational. You might also want to write all those awful, agonizing, angry feelings down in a letter to your ex. Don't worry—you're not going to send it. No, this letter is strictly for your eyes only. So go ahead, get nasty. Tell him how he was bad in bed. Or how you're not going to miss his sloppy kisses or his snoring. Or how he was just a big jerk toward the end. In fact, call him every name in the book! This is your chance to spew all the things you never got to say but really need to get off your chest. You can write your letter in your breakup recovery journal or just on regular paper that you will then seal in an envelope marked "My Big Breakup Letter" and put away for safekeeping (or at least until the urge to send it subsides).

Stick It to Him

After you've trashed him online, written him a vicious letter, and donated his stuff to a good cause, I want you to get out your journal, sit down in a favorite chair, and make a list. This list is for you. It's a list of all the things you've always wanted to do but for whatever reason didn't do while you were with him. It can also include new ways of thinking or behaving that you'd like to put into practice now that Mr. Ex is no longer in your life. Maybe he didn't like to travel. Maybe he didn't want to become a vegetarian. Maybe skydiving wasn't his thing. Or maybe he tried your patience so much that you couldn't be your best self and practice kindness to others. But you know what? None of that matters anymore.

FROM THE **breakup chronicles**

❝After twenty years of marriage, last Christmas my husband told me he needed some space and that this separation would be good for us both. He packed his clothes, kissed me and our kids goodbye, and moved out. Seven days later he told me he had met somebody else. I spent the next few months working out, eating healthy, and working on me. Eventually, I met an amazing man and my kids and I are very happy. As for my ex? He's eating his heart out. Ladies, the best revenge is definitely success!❞

—*Janice*

It's time to put your needs, your wants, and your desires first. It's time to make your new and improved life list, a list of all the things you want to do now that you're free from that *going nowhere* relationship (and lost 170-plus pounds of dead weight). This list is going to be way better than any sinister scheme or revenge fantasy you could possibly dream up. Why? Because this list is all about celebrating you and your amazing new life—a life that is going to be so much better now that Mr. Ex is out of the picture.

So what are you waiting for? Start your life list right now. Need some ideas? Here's my life list. Feel free to borrow from it.

Lisa's New-and-Improved Life List
Things I'm now footloose and fancy-free to do (and be!)

1. Go to Greece (*finally!*).
2. Cut my hair super short and sassy.
3. Take that book-writing class.
4. Spend the summer in Montana.
5. Buy my first home.
6. Be a better friend.
7. Practice patience.
8. Do one nice thing for someone else every day (or at least once a week!).

Red Rover, Red Rover, Send All His Friends Over

After a breakup, you not only lose your ex, you also run the risk of losing some of your mutual friends, and that can make the breakup even more devastating. In times like these, we're likely to take desperate action. Like a politician in an election year, we campaign for our cause. We'll plot, scheme, and possibly even exaggerate what happened to gain sympathy votes. We test the water with friends, acquaintances, and anyone our friends and acquaintances can reach by phone or e-mail.

Do you know what he did?
Did you hear how he dumped her?
He didn't even leave her rent money!

Forget dignity. We'll mud-sling with the best of them just to make sure we still get invited to our favorite holiday parties, still have access to the awesome summer house in Palm Springs or Palm Beach or the Hamptons, and don't have to delete any more numbers from our cell phone. And if we tarnish our ex's reputation along the way? So be it. It's just part of the breakup package, right?

Wrong. Waging an all-out war with your ex over who gets to keep which friends requires far too much of your fabulous energy, energy that is better suited to helping you heal your broken heart and move on. The truth is, your real friends will stick by you. Maybe not all of them (and maybe you'll be surprised by which ones jump ship for your ex's dinghy), but your real true-blue friends will support you through this breakup. They'll call to make sure you're okay. They'll take you out to dinner. They'll send you a reassuring e-mail when you least expect it.

After a particularly painful breakup of mine, I was shocked when my ex's former roommates offered to help me move out of our joint apartment. I couldn't believe they weren't taking his side (and kicking me to the curb in the process). I couldn't believe they still wanted to be my friends. To this day, they are two of my oldest and dearest male friends. And until that breakup, I had no idea I could count on them. (Thanks, Jim and Brett!)

The Flip Side

And then there was the time I was going through my Big Breakup when my friend's husband started inviting my ex over for game night with the guys. They had never even been friends while we were dating. They didn't even have each other's phone numbers. But after the Big Breakup, they suddenly became e-mail buddies. I was devastated and took immediate action, calling my friend's husband and asking him to respect my feelings. I'm not sure if he ever understood, but he did stop inviting my ex over for game night. And that was what ultimately mattered to me.

FROM THE **breakup chronicles**

" My friends don't understand why I'm having such a hard time getting over my ex. They tell me I talk about him way too much and that I'm obsessing about the breakup, which happened a couple months back. They just don't seem to understand how hard this is for me!**"**

—*Hannah*

If you feel like a friend is crossing the line with your ex, be brave enough and bold enough to call them on it. Or if your friends are telling you to *just get over it already*, you may need to re-educate them on what it means to be a true friend. They may not even know they're doing something wrong. They may have forgotten how hard it is to go through a breakup. They may need you to remind them. You may even become closer friends as a result of your bravery!

Double-Dating after Getting Dumped

As for the friends you made as a couple (especially the coupled-up friends you made as a couple), well, they may be casualties of your breakup. If all you ever did together were couple-oriented activities, then what do you really have in common with them now that you're no longer part of that couple? If, on the other hand, you're wondering how to salvage a friendship with your ex's best friend's girlfriend (or anyone else in your ex's life), that's another story.

FROM THE **breakup chronicles**

"My ex and I had been together since high school. After seven years, I knew he wasn't right for me. And he knew it, too. So even though the breakup was hard, we agreed it was for the best. The hardest part was breaking the news to our families, who were very close. There was a period of time when things were awkward, but I'm happy to say that I still have a friendship with them. We send each other holiday cards and when I come to town, I'll have lunch with them. We found a way to still be in each other's lives without making it about a relationship that was over.**"**

—*Kate*

First, ask yourself this important question: Are you trying to maintain the friendship so that you can still have access to your ex's life? Or is your desire to maintain a friendship based on the fact that you genuinely enjoy that person? If you're just trying to hang onto your ex, don't bother. That's not exactly grounds for maintaining a friendship with someone. But if you chose the latter, maintaining a friendship *can* be possible. You may need to set up some new friendship ground rules, like the two of you can never talk about your ex or anyone associated with your ex. And you may not want to include this person in your Boo-Hoo Crew if you're concerned about him or her reporting back to your ex. But that's really your call.

Family Matters

Friends are one thing, but family is another. While some of your ex's family members are easy to break up with (no more excruciating/dutiful visits at the holidays), others are a little more difficult. Maybe his sister became one of your best friends. Or his dad was always so sweet to you. Or you and his mom bonded over his baby pictures. As nice as it would be to maintain the love between you and your ex's family, it's very difficult to do. You need to realize that as much as they may care about you, they're going to put your ex's needs first. And that's not in your best interest.

FROM THE DEADBEAT BOYFRIEND FILES

Think your breakup was bad?
Check out what this clueless cad did . . .

" It's been just two weeks now since my jerk husband left me high and dry with no money and a stack of bills. I feel like he emotionally murdered me. While I'm left wondering not only how to pick up the pieces and move on but also how to financially stay afloat, he has already moved on and shows no signs of remorse or concern for the pain he has caused me.**"**

—*Cyndi*

Let's all send Cyndi our strength and energy. She really needs it right now!

After a breakup, it's probably best to distance yourself not only from your ex, but from his family as well. Think of it this way. You and your ex may have seen this breakup coming, but your families probably didn't. They may need time to grieve. They may not have been ready to break up with you or your ex. And just like you, their formula for a breakup timeline says that Time + Distance = Moving on. So give them the same chance you deserve—the opportunity to move on. If you're meant to stay in each other's lives, you can always reconnect once your hearts have healed.

Breakup Bitterness

Raise your hand if you're feeling a little bitter about your breakup. (Go ahead, raise it high with pride!) Whether you got dumped or did the dumping, chances are you have moments of post-breakup bitterness. You may feel like you wasted time in the relationship. Or that you were made to look like a fool. Or that you can't believe how he treated you in the end. (Some people can be downright nasty during a breakup.)

WHAT'S ON A BITTER GIRL'S BOOKSHELF?

BitterGirl: Getting Over Getting Dumped, by Annabel Griffiths, Alison Lawrence, and Mary Francis Moore

If you're gonna be bitter, why not bask in your bitterness with this outrageously fun book? The Bitter Girls will show you how to use your bitterness for good and still move on!

In their own words: "Becoming a bittergirl is an evolutionary process. You don't just wake up one morning, evening gown on, tiara in place, martini in hand, and announce to the world that you're a bittergirl. There are rites of passage you must go through."

breakup secret #6
It's okay to be bitter. In fact, it's good!

If you're feeling bitter, don't despair. You can channel that bitterness into something amazing. Actually, you can channel any negative breakup emotion into something positive like added incentive to lose ten pounds, go back to school, or buy your first condo. Think of your breakup bitterness as your new best friend. Together, you're going to be that much more motivated to move on from your ex and do something even more incredible with your life!

The Tough-Love Truth

After your Big Breakup, you may still have questions. They might go something like this:

Is my ex still thinking about me?

Does he miss me?

Does he want me back?

Or is he completely over me?

While you may not be ready to hear it, the only answer I have is this: Maybe.

Feel better? I didn't think so. But that's the only honest answer.

Here's another tough-love truth. You can continue asking yourself these questions until you're blue in the face, or you can face facts:

Fact It doesn't matter what your ex is thinking anymore.

Fact Love him or hate him, your ex is now your ex.

Fact You may never have the answers to all those questions swirling around in your head.

Fact It's still over.

But my ex was a great guy, you might be saying right about now. *I'll never meet anyone as wonderful as he was!* And up he goes on the pedestal again.

RECOVERY ℞

In a funk? Spice up your routine by purchasing a new perfume, scented body lotion (preferably a new scent), or new aromatherapy candles. You'll be surprised at how life-changing introducing a new scent can be!

Once more I'm here to point out the tough-love truth. I didn't write this book for your ex. And you didn't pick up this book to be reminded about how amazing your ex was. This book isn't about your ex. This book is about you. About how amazing you are. In case you've forgotten, you are pretty magnificent! And that magnificence didn't suddenly leave you when your ex did. No, your Fabulous Factor is still here. It may just be hidden under your wrinkled pajamas, uncombed hair, and that ice cream–induced sugar coma. But in case you've forgotten, you're in a slump. You're allowed.

Assessing Your Fabulous Factor

Even though you're mid-slump, I have an assignment for you. Grab your journal and a pen. Find a clean page and write the numbers one through ten down the side of it. And now, write down ten magnificent things about you. They can range from silly to serious to quite remarkable. No one other than you will ever see the list, so feel free to write down whatever you want. This list is to remind you of your Fabulous Factor whenever you're in doubt.

What are you waiting for? Get started! Need some ideas? Take a look at my Fabulous Factor list:

Lisa's Fabulous Factor

1. I'm an excellent parallel parker.
2. I make heavenly chocolate chip cookies.
3. People tell me I have an infectious laugh.
4. I throw a great party.
5. My calves are pretty sexy.
6. I'm fun to travel with.
7. My margaritas rock!
8. I've perfected the art of the nap.
9. I love my tattoos.
10. I have fantastic friends.

Once you've finished your Fabulous Factor list, look it over. Does it make you feel fabulous? It should! I want you to hold onto this list. We'll be adding to it in later chapters.

Now that you know the rules of post-breakup behavior, you're much better equipped to handle your own Big Breakup. It's not always going to be easy (but then again, it won't always be devastatingly difficult, either). As a

Big Breakup survivor, you reserve the right to behave inappropriately at times. You're allowed to be a mess. This is one of the few times in your life when rebounding is forgivable. When being bitter is a good thing! But revenge comes with repercussions, and fighting over friends isn't worth your time or energy. Finally, when in doubt, refer to your Fabulous Factor list. Feel free to add to it. This is just the beginning of rediscovering your own fabulousness.

between-chapter *check-in*

Ready to check in? Write down your five emotions here or in your journal (you can have good and bad ones!).

Compare this list with your previous lists on pages 26 and 47. Are you noticing any patterns developing? Anything you can work on in the coming weeks? (You're doing just great—keep up the amazing work!)

DATE

CHAPTER FOUR
the post-breakUP roller coaster

right about now, you may be hitting your post-breakup stride. You've made it through an entire week without crying at work, are back at the gym and feeling good, and are probably only wearing your pajamas at night. You may have even graduated from the entire pint of Ben & Jerry's to just a spoonful or two when you get home from work or before bed. At this point you may be thinking, *Wow, this breakup slump stuff is easy.*

And then it happens.

It's Friday night and for the first time since you can remember, you don't have any plans. Saturday afternoon rolls around and you have hours to fill with no one to fill them with. You wake up in the middle of the night, hear a strange noise, and realize that it must be a burglar because Mr. Ex is no longer there to make his middle-of-the-night trip to the bathroom, accidentally step on the cat, and cause a ruckus.

73

And because you've been doing so well in your post-Big Breakup recovery, your Boo-Hoo Crew is off the clock. They're no longer sleeping in shifts with the phone next to their beds. They're all out, probably on dates, possibly meeting the men of their dreams, and you're home alone. At this point, the panic sets in. And it hits you—the thing nobody warns you about before the breakup. You've got too much free time on your hands. That can be the kiss of death!

With too much time on your hands, you can easily get into trouble. You could obsess about your ex. Your mind could spiral out of control, asking those questions you know you're not supposed to—and will never know the answers to anyway. The *whys* and *what ifs* take hold of your brain. You unsuccessfully fight the urge to put your ex back on that pedestal, knocking yourself to the ground in the process. At times like this, you may convince yourself that you'll never date again. That all your friends will meet their Mr. Rights and your ex, well, he's probably already found someone new and is on the fast track to *happily ever after*. But you—you'll never meet anyone good again—ever!

RECOVERY ℞

Tired of takeout or frozen dinners? Treat yourself to a home-cooked meal complete with wine, dessert, and ambience (light some candles, listen to relaxing music). Or, if cooking for one feels cumbersome, order takeout from your favorite restaurant or pizza place. Just be sure to eat on the good plates. You deserve to feel pampered so go ahead, live a little!

Stop. Don't go there.

You know how sometimes your computer acts funky and you have to reboot? Well, now's the time to reboot your brain. And you have to accept that there are going to be times during your slump when you feel this way. As awful, uncomfortable, and panic-inducing as it can be, it's not the end of the world. You will get through this. For the moment, you just need to breathe and reboot.

Another Potential Setback

To help fill your time, you're on an obsessive cleaning streak. You've gone from sweeping and mopping the floors to reorganizing your filing cabinet and clearing out closets. Somewhere between your high school yearbook and your college diploma, there it is. Your favorite photo of the two of you together. Or that "get well soon" card and the flowers you dried and forgot about, from when you first started dating and had that terrible cold. Happy memories come flooding back, and all of a sudden you're struck with the urge to call your ex. Just to say hi, right?

FROM THE DEADBEAT BOYFRIEND FILES

Think your breakup was bad?
Check out what this clueless cad did . . .

"I was in a four-year relationship with a guy whom I fell for in an instant. I was six months pregnant with his baby when I found out he was hiding a serious drug problem from me. I stuck by him, helping him through detox. Then he got into harder drugs and started cheating with a fellow addict. I'm left feeling so ashamed for putting up with his bad behavior. I have no idea what I'll tell my child about her father.**"**

—*Krista*

Whether she knows it or not, Krista is better off without this cheating addict. And so is her baby!

Wrong. Don't do it. You've come too far to take such a disastrous U-turn in your progress. Instead, go for a run, or phone a friend, or take a long hot bubble bath until the urge to reach out and touch your ex subsides. You owe it to yourself and to your recovery to stay strong. (And don't forget to reboot that brain of yours!)

Now (or at least once it's daylight) would be a good time to regroup the Boo-Hoo Crew for a post-breakup recovery powwow. Once you've gathered the girls, together you should come up with a list of at least twenty things you can do if and when you find yourself with too much free time on your hands and nobody's around to help fill it. (Or for those times when you come across a memento that has you reaching for the phone and dialing your ex's digits without thinking.) Yes, your Boo-Hoo Crew should still be on call in case of emergencies (like running into your ex while he's on a date, when you've tried everything but still find that you've lost all resolve and are about to call your ex, or just when you're feeling especially blue), but now's the time in your post-breakup recovery to incorporate self-reliance.

Fact: Your girlfriends have lives. You should get one, too.

So open your journal and make your list of things to do. It should consist of activities you already love doing, things you've never done but would love to try, and things that make you feel good about yourself. Here's mine—the list that helped me through my Big Breakup.

Lisa's List

Twenty things to do when I've got too much free time on my hands:

1. Get a pedicure.
2. Walk on the beach.

3. Go to a movie.
4. Take a bubble bath.
5. Write in my journal.
6. Get a massage.
7. Go for a drive up the coast.
8. Take a Pilates class.
9. Practice deep breathing for five minutes.
10. Buy more Ben & Jerry's.
11. Make a collage of my ideal life.
12. Listen to live music.
13. Snuggle with my cats.
14. Sign up for salsa dancing classes (finally!).
15. Go hiking.
16. Buy myself something pretty.
17. Plan a road trip.
18. Buy and flip through celebrity gossip magazines.
19. Relax in the Jacuzzi.
20. Remind myself that this, too, will pass.

Were you able to come up with twenty things? If not, keep working on it. Ten is a good start, but twenty is better. And be sure to keep your list handy. You never know when you'll need it. You might even want to tear it out and tack it up on your refrigerator to serve as a visual reminder of what you need to focus on right now.

Mission Possible

Because there will be times when you question your ability to survive the Big Breakup, you're gonna need another little reminder of your progress. Your mission, should you choose to accept it, is to go out and purchase one item that is symbolic of your post–Big Breakup recovery. The purpose of this item is to serve as a visual cue when you're feeling blue. It should be something to remind you of your Fabulous Factor when you may otherwise forget. It doesn't have to be expensive. It can be an item of clothing that accentuates your curves or cleavage or calves, a new set of wine glasses to help you toast your new life, or even a new set of sheets that Mr. Ex will never sleep on. Whether it's frivolous or functional is up to you. It's just gotta be something that makes you feel fantastic. For me, it was a red feather boa that I hung on my bedroom door. It was one of the last things I saw every night before I went to bed and one of the first things I saw when I woke up. If I was having a particularly mopey Saturday afternoon, I'd wrap that boa around my neck, turn on some music, and dance around my living room. Sometimes after a difficult day at work, I'd come home, put on my PJs, drape the boa around me, and enjoy a glass of wine. Or if I was particularly stressed out about paying all the bills by myself, I'd break out the boa and write those checks with flair. For me, my breakup recovery symbol didn't need a hefty price tag. It just needed to remind me that with or without a man, especially Mr. Ex, I would always be fabulous! Chances are, you've already got a breakup recovery symbol in mind. Now it's time to go out there and get it.

Pitfalls of Post–Big Breakup Recovery

There will be times when you make great strides in your recovery. Times when you feel healthy and strong and happy with your new life. But then there will also be times when you backslide. At these times, you will feel lost and alone—like the Big Breakup *just happened,* even if it was over weeks or months ago. Somewhere between all that free time, your forward motion, and the inevitable backsliding, you may even discover that, gulp, *you miss your ex.*

breakup secret #7
It's perfectly normal to miss your ex.

That's another thing no one tells you before the breakup. Just because your relationship is over doesn't mean your feelings are.

Missing your ex is one thing. Contacting your ex is another (see Chapter 1 for a refresher course in Ex Etiquette if needed). You're allowed to miss your ex. After all, you loved him. He was a big part of your life—of course you're going to miss him now that he's gone!

The good news is if you still harbor feelings for your ex or you have moments (or days) when you miss him, you're perfectly normal. Of course, if you're completely over your ex, that's fantastic, too! That's the thing about breaking up—there's no one perfect way to handle it. Just as your relationship was unique, your breakup recovery will be unique, too.

FROM THE breakup chronicles

"I couldn't believe it when my ex broke up with me. He was just so callous. But you know what? I did my best to accept it and move on. In the beginning it was hard. I fought the urge to contact him or to try to get him back. I survived. And now I can see that it was the *best* thing for me. I thank him for that and now I am happier than ever. I was set free!**"**

—*Veronica*

So when those difficult post-breakup feelings pop up, remember this: As intense as the pain can sometimes feel, as much as you may or may not miss your ex, as challenging as managing all that free time can be, all of it is temporary. As time moves on, so will you. That's the beauty of a breakup, even the Big Breakup. You do eventually move on. And your life is so much better for having gone through these difficult times.

While it's perfectly natural and normal to miss your ex, I *know* there are things you're not gonna miss. I want to turn your attention to those things for a minute. Sure, it's easy to put your ex on a pedestal after it's all over and remember all those wonderful qualities he had. But remember all those annoying habits? You know the ones—the things that drove you nuts when you were together. Right here and now, I want you to write down five things in your journal that you are *not* going to miss about Mr. Ex. Seriously, write them down now. Need some help? Here's my list:

1. His mood swings
2. His money problems
3. His dad
4. Football season (and the moodiness after his team lost)
5. His emotional unavailability

Did you come up with five things? If ten come to mind, write down ten! When you're done, look at your list for a minute and congratulate yourself. You no longer have to put up with any of those annoying things. And whenever you're feeling blue or really missing your ex, I want you to look at this list and remember why it's good he's gone.

Once again, let me remind you—congratulations on your breakup! You really dodged a bullet there, didn't you? (Just look at that list, and I think you'll agree.)

FROM THE **breakup chronicles**

❝ Once I went cold turkey, I used the time that I had previously spent fretting about Mr. Ex to work on my own issues. Like why I felt so horrid about myself, and how on earth did I expect some guy to fix it. Each day without Mr. Ex I got a little better, a little stronger, a little healthier. Until soon he was just a word at the tip of my tongue, familiar and yet forgotten. ❞

—*Nina*

Okay—you've identified twenty ways to fill your free time and found the symbol of your breakup recovery. Those things are easy enough, but you may still find that even with your list of your ex's annoying habits, you're obsessing (slightly) about him. Even with all the great strides you're making in your own life, you may still miss him.

And that's okay. I've got a fabulous secret weapon to share with you!

The Six-Month Secret

If I told you there was only one thing you had to do to get over your breakup, would you do it?

Think about that for a minute. You have to do only *one thing*, and you're guaranteed to get over the pain of your breakup that much quicker. This one thing will make all the difference, not only in how you handle the breakup but also in how quickly you move on. Sound too good to be true? It's not! And that's what's so fabulous about it. It is time-tested, practically foolproof.

Are you ready? Here it is. All you have to do to ensure an easier post-breakup recovery is this: Stop thinking about your ex.

Now I know what you might be thinking—I've just asked you to do the impossible. But I haven't, and that's the brilliance of the secret weapon! When I told you to stop thinking about your ex, I didn't mean you could never have another thought about him. That would be practically impossible. What I meant was that the key to getting through your breakup as smoothly as possible is to put the focus on *you*— your healing and your new life, *not* on your ex and his new life. The sooner you let go of wondering where he is, who he's with (*stop that!*), and what he's doing, the sooner you'll be able to move on.

But here's the catch (and I think it's equally fabulous!). Only you have the power to do this. If you give yourself permission here and now—and I mean *today*—to let go of your ex and move on from this breakup, you will do it. And six months from now, just imagine where you'll be.

Reasons Why You Might Not Want to Let Go

If the idea of letting go of your ex excites you, congratulations! You're extraordinarily brave and bold and ready to move on. And you're free to skip over this next part. However, if the idea completely terrifies you, you're not alone. In fact, you're perfectly normal. Walking away from a significant other, even after a breakup, may be one of the hardest things you'll ever do.

The following is a list of reasons why you might be resisting the need to let go. Once we pinpoint the reason, we can identify your breakup persona and figure out how to let go and move on for good.

You Still Love Him

Plain and simple, you're still in love with your ex. Take heart, my friend. You're not the first fab female—and you definitely won't be the last—to harbor feelings for an ex. Your breakup persona is the Hopeless Romantic. The good news is that you'll definitely find love again. And with the right guy, your heart will be in good hands. A word of caution, though—Hopeless Romantics have a tendency to hold on to relationships long after they're over. And in doing so, you just might run into your ex's new girlfriend. Double ouch! Walk away, Hopeless Romantic, while your dignity's still intact.

CELEBRITY HOPELESS ROMANTIC: *Jennifer Lopez*

She loves and leaves big, and then quickly moves on to someone new. Has this hopeless romantic moved on from her past, learned her lessons, and finally found her match in hubby #3 Marc Anthony?

J-Lo to *People* magazine on the Bennifer debacle: "If it wasn't for that experience, who knows what I would have done, who I would have been—hopefully still a nice person but maybe not in as good a place as I am now."

You're Worried about Him

Are you worried about how Mr. Ex will function without you? Worried that his fragile state has been made more so by the breakup? You're not alone. Your breakup persona is the Caretaker. Let's be clear—there's nothing wrong with taking care of someone (as long as it's the right someone). But if you're a magnet for every stray guy who's out there, you're in for a lifetime of romantic pain and suffering. And Caretakers beware—ex-boyfriends are notorious for taking advantage of your good nature. D.N.R. (do not resuscitate).

CELEBRITY CARETAKER: *Britney Spears*

With all the fame and fortune a girl could want, the only thing missing from Ms. Spears's life was someone to share it with. But in hooking up with hubby K-Fed, the world watched this pop princess go from top of the world to bargain basement in her role as the ultimate caretaker (and sugar mama). After two years of marriage (and practicing proper breakup etiquette), Britney called it quits just before the 2006 holiday season. And while her post-breakup behavior was as questionable as her choice in a husband (panty-less partying with Paris?!), by the time you read this, let's hope Britney's well on her way to a remarkable comeback!

Britney on her own bizarre post-breakup behavior: "Every move I make at this point has been magnified more than I expected, and I probably did take my newfound freedom a little too far. . . . I look forward to a new year, new music, and a new me." (We do, too!)

You're Not Sure It's Really Over

Are you still holding out hope that your relationship isn't totally over? Do you have lots of unanswered questions and find yourself regularly asking *Why?* Do these unanswered questions paralyze you, making it impossible to move on? Your breakup persona is the Crime Scene Investigator. CSIs tend to linger too long at the breakup scene. They may even muddy the evidence by going back and sleeping with their ex after all is said and done. But this only leads to more questions, and it's risky behavior to be avoided at all costs. If you're a CSI, the best thing you can do for your heart is accept that not all of your questions will be answered and give yourself permission to move on anyway.

CELEBRITY CSI: *Sienna Miller*

They were on again, they were off again. This girl changed her mind about Jude Law more often than she changed her hairstyle! But it looks like this Crime Scene Investigator may have finally accepted that she'll never get the answers she was looking for from her nanny-nibbling Casanova. Good riddance!

Sienna during a moment of clarity: "Just stay single. Stick together with your girlies."

Sienna in cloudier times: "I have met a few Casanovas I like and a few I have not liked—and I hope to meet a few more." (Isn't one Casanova enough for a lifetime?!)

You're Afraid No One Else Will Come Along

This is probably the most dangerous breakup belief of all because it sells you and your fabulousness completely short! If you feel this way, your persona is the Pessimist. Pessimists tend to settle for less than they deserve in relationships because they haven't fully discovered their own magnificence. They gravitate toward relationships with people they think can help them or make them happy. But the only person who can ultimately make you happy is—you guessed it—*you*! If you're a Pessimist, the best thing you can do post–Big Breakup is take some much-needed time for self nurturing, focus on fixing the cracks in your self-esteem, and learn to love yourself as you are. (And stay very far away from your ex!)

CELEBRITY PESSIMISTS:

Halle Berry, Jenny McCarthy

Whether they thought they were settling for less or not, both of these ladies have proven that life after a fairy-tale marriage that ended in divorce is sweeter than staying in a relationship that's no longer working. From post-breakup career successes to hot beaus to looking sexier than ever, these ladies make movin' on look amazing! Take a page from their post-breakup playbooks and discover the joys of celebrating your own fabulousness (and in the process becoming an optimist).

Here's Jenny McCarthy on what she learned from her divorce from ex-hubby film director John Asher: "What happened was I realized I fell in love with a man, a fantasy of who I thought this man was and not really who he is. I think a lot of people go into a relationship thinking, *Oh, this man will complete me. This man will make me whole and happy.* You have to go into a relationship already complete and already happy. I was looking everywhere else for it and really thought that he would offer that. I was getting so angry at him for seven years, going *How can you not complete me or make me happy?* It's because I wasn't."

Your Biological Clock Is Tick, Tick, Ticking

Afraid to let go of your ex because your biological clock is ticking away? If you think that time is running out on your chance to get married or have a baby, then your breakup persona is Chicken Little. The good news is that just like Chicken Little, not only is the sky not falling, but you are *not* running out of time. Just look around and you'll see that women are getting married and having babies well into their forties. And don't forget, adoption and surrogacy are fantastic alternatives to good old-fashioned pregnancy. The thing I always remind my fab female friends is that if you want to get married, all you have to do is go out there and find some guy who's looking to get married, too. There's no guarantee that you'll be happy, but you will be married. Instead, why not set your sights on a more satisfying goal, like creating a happy life for your single self? You're much more likely to attract a healthy and happy partner if you're healthy and happy on your own. In the meantime, a word of caution: Ex-boyfriends love to prey on Chicken Little's paranoia. Don't give in (and don't give up—you're far too fabulous for that!).

CELEBRITY CHICKEN LITTLE: Teri Hatcher

The fabulous desperate housewife was once in an unhappy marriage that was so sexless she claims in her book *Burnt Toast* that she knows exactly when her daughter was conceived because it was the only time she and her husband had sex that year. Fortunately for this Chicken Little, she walked away from her broken marriage, embraced single motherhood, and found inner peace as well as multiple career successes. A winning formula for sure!

Here's Teri on monogamy after marriage: "I did not marry bad guys, but ultimately I didn't make good choices. . . . Now I want sex: trusting, deep, fabulous, open, wild, crazy sex, with the same person, over and over." (You go, girl!)

Deciphering Your Breakup Persona

The good thing about identifying your breakup persona is that it helps you better understand why you might not want to move on from your ex. It also helps you better understand how you handle a breakup. And now that we've identified where you might be having trouble in your post-breakup recovery, we can talk about why it's *still* time to move on.

Fact Like it or not, your relationship is over.

Fact You don't have to know *Why?* to move on (so stop making yourself crazy!).

Fact The sooner you accept the breakup, the sooner you'll move on (and you deserve to move on!).

The Awful (and Amazing) Truth

Some of you may be thinking that you're still not quite ready to let go of your ex. That there is a certain amount of comfort in holding on to him and the rubble that remains of your relationship (also known as getting stuck in your slump). And then there are those of you who are ready to move on from the slump. Ready to leave behind Mr. Ex and who you were with him. And others still may be faltering, wondering which group you fall into.

FROM THE **breakup chronicles**

"After staying with someone too long, ignoring my instincts, and being made a fool of, this is what I have learned. Put yourself and your needs first. Don't ever give up your dignity. And after a breakup, focus on the future not the past because the past is gone. But the future, the future is ours!**"**

—*Heidi*

You don't have to be 100 percent certain that you're ready to take the leap. I wasn't sure I was ready to take the leap when I did. But I decided, and I hope you will, too, to be brave and bold and to choose my own personal well-being over my concerns and worries for someone I was no longer in a relationship with.

Ultimately, you have a choice. It's up to you. In six months, do you want to still be thinking about your ex and possibly his new girlfriend, or do you want to be living and loving your new life, with nothing but a fleeting thought of your ex and an afterthought of *Thank God*? Only you know the answer, but I hope you'll make the decision that has your best interests at heart.

Food for Thought

In just six months, you can do a lot, including:

○ Lose thirty pounds.
○ Train for a marathon.
○ Learn a new language.
○ Buy and move into your own home.
○ Plan and take a super fabulous vacation.
○ Be completely over your ex.
○ Fall in love with someone new (just make sure you're not rebounding!).

between-chapter *check-in*

Time to check in by recording your five
emotions here or in your journal. Don't
forget that you can include both good *and*
bad feelings (or somewhere in between!).
Just be honest about how you're feeling
right now.

Compare this list with your previous
lists on pages 26, 47, and 71. What kind
of progress are you noticing? Any areas
where you're struggling?

Whether you know it or not, you're doing
just fine. Keep going!

DATE

_____

_____

_____

_____

_____

CHAPTER FIVE
kicking the habit
aka breaking up with your breakUP

have you noticed that lately when you talk about the breakup, it's starting to feel like it happened to someone else? (Whaddaya know? No more tears!) There's a reason for that. You've done the work. Put in the hours. You've been on the emotional roller coaster, experienced your fair share of mourning, gotten down and dirty in celebrating your slump. And don't forget the fact that you're no longer coupled up with what's-his-name. Right about now, that probably feels more and more like a blessing than just a cruel twist of fate.

Maybe it's the new wardrobe, your new and improved outlook on life, or the ex-boyfriend bonfire that did the trick (or any combination thereof), but *wouldn't you know it*, you're starting to feel like your old self again (only better, of course!). You're probably even getting used to the idea of being on your own. Whereas sleeping in the middle of the bed used to feel borderline blasphemous, it's now a nightly celebration of your newly single self. (And if you're a total rock star, you might just be sleeping diagonally!)

But as you mentally prepare to break up with your breakup, you may still hesitate, wondering *What's next?* Well, what's next is pretty fantastic. And it's going to get you one step closer to Part Two of this book, also known as Movin' On. What's next? Whether you know it or not, it's time to dump your slump!

Did you just sit up a little straighter and smile? Or did you sit back in your chair and furrow your forehead? Either way, don't worry. Remember, we're in this together. Before we go about the business of dumping your slump, we're going to first determine your slump-dumper personality. Take the quiz on the following page to help us figure out how ready and willing you are to break up with your breakup. Once you complete the quiz, read on.

Slump-Dumping Styles

Now that we've assessed your slump-dumping style and determined how willing you are to breakup with your breakup, it's time to help you over that last hurdle and into movin' on mode! Here's how:

If you're cautious

Cautious slump-dumpers tend to be somewhat shy and reserved. When it comes to relationships, they often find themselves in the passenger seat while their partner seems to drive all the choices, decisions, and actions—*including* the breakup. If you rate as a cautious SD, you may be hesitant to break up with your breakup.

Slump-Dumper Personality Quiz

When it comes to change, which of the following life changes are you most comfortable with?

1. A change of clothes
2. A new hairstyle
3. Relocating to a new city

What do you consider the ultimate splurge?

1. The chocolate lava cake at your favorite restaurant
2. That red leather jacket you've been eyeing
3. A two-week trip to Europe by yourself

What's a typical Saturday night for a single gal like you?

1. Renting movies at home
2. Cocktails with your girlfriends at the lounge with the notoriously cute bartenders
3. Between the outdoor Jazzfest, the independent film festival, and the three club openings, who can decide?

What's the most adventuresome thing you would try?

1. A double shot in your latte or mocha
2. Taking a salsa dancing class solo
3. Bungee jumping or skydiving (or both!)

And finally... What's the longest period of time you've gone without a boyfriend in your adult life?

1. Six weeks
2. Six months to one year
3. A couple of years

Slump-Dumper Personality Quiz scoring

Okay, that last question doesn't have much to do with your slump-dumping style. But it's definitely something to think about as you prepare to break up with your breakup. (We'll address how comfortable you are being on your own in the section titled "Embracing Your Single Self," on page 97.)

Scoring: Now take a look at your answers to the quiz questions. If you found that most of your answers were 1, then your slump-dumping (SD) style is cautious. If most of your answers were 2, then your slump-dumping style is fiery. And if you mostly answered 3, then your slump-dumping style is fearless. Regardless of how you answered, read the descriptions on these pages and see which one you most relate to. Once we've identified your slump-dumper personality, I've got some tips and tools to help you break up with your breakup.

Fear of the unknown has somehow convinced you that it's easier to stay in the slump than to move through it. You have this crazy notion that if you just hide under the covers for a few more months, heck, maybe even the rest of the year, no one will notice. But that just won't do! As scary as it is, cautious slump-dumpers need to summon up their inner strength, look themselves in the mirror, and remind themselves of their inner fabulousness.

Revisiting your Fabulous Factor list should help. In fact, if you're a cautious SD, I want you to add three more things to your Fabulous Factor list right now. I know it's not your style to brag or boast, but I'm giving you permission to embrace your own magnificence. Actually, that's an order. So go for it! Once you do, dumping your slump will be easy.

And when in doubt, don't be afraid to ask your Boo-Hoo Crew for help. (That's what friends are for!)

Cautious Slump-Dumper Cheat Sheet

Before moving on, cautious SDs must do the following:

1. Stop hiding under the covers (come out, come out, wherever you are!).
2. Embrace your inner fab female.
3. Add three new things to your Fabulous Factor list.

If you're fiery

If you naturally lean toward being a fiery slump-dumper, then you probably also regularly find yourself the center of attention. And while being the life of the party rocks, we both know what happens when the party's over. It's back to Slumpville for you, oh fabulous one. That's just the nature of your yin-yang over-the-top personality. One minute you're filled with joy, the next you're an emotional wreck. And the only surefire way to balance the emotional pendulum associated with the fiery female's slump is to get real. That can be uncomfortable because it means you have to take a long hard look in the mirror.

Unlike cautious SDs, who need to embrace their inner fabulousness, you need to get *beyond* your own fabulousness and take a peek at what's underneath it. Chances are you're like other fiery females—afraid that being single too long means you just might be single forever. And while that's probably not going to happen, you need to ask yourself whether that would be so bad. If you're as fiery as you let on, wouldn't your life be equally incredible with or without a boyfriend? (Again, I'll address this particular concern in more depth later in the chapter. For now, just acknowledge that you *are* spectacular and that you *will* survive and thrive on your own!)

Fiery Slump-Dumper Cheat Sheet

Before moving on, fiery SDs must take these steps:

1. Balance your emotional pendulum.
2. Make peace with the fear of being single (it's not the same as being alone or lonely).
3. Celebrate your single status (it's a blessing, not a curse!).

If you're fearless

If you're a fearless slump-dumper, you may not need any help dumping your slump. After all, life is one big adventure for you! You live out loud and have probably been waiting for permission to dump your slump for some time now (not that you normally ask for permission). But you need to remember that even though you live life to the fullest, there will be times when you could really just use a hug. These are the times when you need to ask your Boo-Hoo Crew for help. Asking for help will be your biggest stumbling block as you move on, Adventure Girl. It's time to realize that leaning on others from time to time is not a sign of weakness—it's a show of strength!

Fearless Slump-Dumper Cheat Sheet

Before moving on, fearless SDs must do the following:

1. Learn to ask for help.
2. Practice patience (it won't always be smooth sailing!).
3. Celebrate your inner fearlessness (it's definitely a gift!).

Embracing Your Single Self

Of course being single and fabulous takes work. And there are times when it takes courage, too. Which is why now is the perfect time to borrow a page or two from the post-breakup playbooks of some famous females including Mariah Carey, Meg Ryan, and Jane Fonda. What do these leading ladies know that you might not yet know? That it's much better to be single and fabulous than unhappily hooked up. That it's never too late to be true to yourself. And that by being true to themselves, these gals have made being single and fabulous look that much more appealing. (And you will, too!)

Think about the courage it took these women to walk away from the high-profile relationships that practically defined them. One was an undiscovered songstress who married the well-connected man who discovered her. Another was America's sweetheart who married a sexy bad-boy actor. And one was a screen icon who married a media mogul. From the fairy-tale courtships to the dreamy weddings to the red carpet relationships, they seemed to have it all. At least that's how we saw it from the outside. But on the inside, things must have been different (and far from perfect!). Over time, the drama deepened. And in the end each famous female discovered the truth about fairy tales—they're not real.

FROM THE **breakup chronicles**

❝ I met and fell in love with this guy who was ten years older than me. At first, everything was great. He treated me like a princess, showered me with love and affection, and even paid off my student loan debt. But then things changed. He became possessive, controlling. At first I was afraid to leave. I didn't know how I'd make it on my own. I now realize that I hadn't been a princess—I'd been a prisoner.**❞**

—Tammy

Not only that, but these famous females also discovered that there *are* things money can't buy, like the perfect relationship or happiness in an unhappy marriage. They may have been surrounded by mansions, millions, and mega-celebrity status, but the best gift these ladies ever received (and you know they got some bling-tastic gifts!) was when they summoned the courage to walk away from the false fairy tale, also known as *not so happily ever after,* and strike out on their own. And unlike other celebrities who routinely jump from relationship to relationship, these wise women proved what you will soon discover if you haven't already—that standing on your own two feet is the ultimate measure of success. (See for yourself!)

Mariah Carey

After her divorce from music producer Tommy Mottola in the late '90s, Mariah's career suffered several setbacks, including getting dropped from her record label, her globally panned performance in the movie *Glitter,* and an alleged emotional breakdown. However, Ms. Mariah persevered, hitting it big once again with her award-winning album *The Emancipation of Mimi* and a hot new body. Love her or hate her, this songbird proves that success comes to those who are true to themselves, and who refuse to play by someone else's rules.

Signature of success Best-selling female vocal artist of all time.

Mariah on her own emancipation "You really have to look inside yourself and find your own inner strength, and say, 'I'm proud of what I am and who I am, and I'm just going to be myself.'"

Meg Ryan

Most of us know her for her perky performances in movies like *When Harry Met Sally, Sleepless in Seattle,* and *You've Got Mail.* Not to mention her high-profile marriage to actor Dennis Quaid (and subsequent divorce amidst rumors of a torrid affair with Aussie actor Russell Crowe). And then Meg all but disappeared from the Hollywood radar. Recently she has reappeared with a new life and a new purpose. Having adopted a baby girl from China, she is using her fame to shine a spotlight on women's issues in Third World countries. In doing so, Meg shows us that while fame can wreak havoc on your personal life, it can also be used for good.

Signature of success Working with the humanitarian group CARE to help women's causes in Third World countries, raising daughter Daisy as a single mother.

What Meg told Oprah about lessons learned after her devastating divorce "There are times in every woman's life where she does need to get out and expand and do all those things that make her the best version of herself."

Jane Fonda

Known for her famous father, antiwar activism, award-winning acting career, and 1980s exercise empire, Ms. Fonda epitomized what the world thought of as a strong and fearless woman. And yet she's been very candid about her struggles with self-esteem and men. Her 2001 divorce from Ted Turner marked a turning point in this leading lady's life. A critically acclaimed autobiography, a return to acting, a renewed spiritual faith, and continued antiwar activism have since followed, proving that it's never too late to be true to yourself (and in the process enjoy a tremendous comeback!).

Signature of success Scene-stealing performance in *Monster-in-Law* and a bestselling autobiography, *My Life So Far.*

Jane on life after her third divorce "Oddly enough, this is the most wonderful period of my life. . . . While sad, divorce doesn't necessarily mean failure. The things which cause us the most pain are also the things we learn most from."

But enough about Mariah, Meg, and Jane. What about you? How are you feeling about your newly single self and the fabulous new life that awaits you? Are you ready to stand on your own two feet and proudly (and loudly) embrace your post–Big Breakup adventure? Or are you still hesitant to break up with your breakup and move on because you're just not sure how you feel about being on your own?

The Single Stigma

Once upon a time, single women everywhere were afraid that being single too long meant they just might be single forever. But today, that's just an antiquated notion in need of a major rewrite. If for some reason you cling to the idea that being single is a punishment you're not sure you can bear, it's time to once again reboot your brain. The truth is, being single is not a life sentence.

It's a state of mind. And it can be an amazing one if you apply your own personal flair to it. Exactly how do you do that? By being the star of your own life story. By not waiting for *some guy* to come along and complete/fix/save you. By tweaking how you look at your life. Instead of viewing your single status as something you have to make the best of, why not look at your life as something to holistically make the most of under any circumstance, whether you're single, dating, married, or whatever? By putting the focus of your life on you—figuring out who you are, and what you want—you take the pressure off of waiting for some external force to fix everything. After all, you're magnificent! Not because you're single or in spite of being single, but just because you are. It's about time you *really* believed it. And you can start by celebrating your current life and the many amazing adventures that are just around the corner. That's what Part Two of this book is all about (we're gonna have so much fun!).

FROM THE DEADBEAT BOYFRIEND FILES

Think your breakup was bad?
Check out what this clueless cad did . . .

"I was engaged to be married in September of 2004. In June, my ex decided that he didn't think it was going to work. We had been together for five years, not to mention everything for the wedding was done and paid for. Plus, we had just bought a house! Five months after what would have been our wedding, he married someone else. Six months later, they had a baby.**"**

—*Bridgette*

Let's congratulate Bridgette on dodging the biggest bullet of her life! (And be sure to give thanks for the one who got away in your life.)

Life Lessons for the Savvy Single

Think about what you'd miss out on if you never went through a breakup—that is, what your life would be like if you were *still* in a relationship with your first boyfriend.

Think about all the lessons you never would have learned without going through that first breakup (and all the ones that followed). And now think about what you might be learning from your Big Breakup (or any breakup) right this very second that you would never have discovered if it hadn't happened. Like the fact that maybe you want to go back to school. Or travel abroad. Or live alone for the first time in your life. Regardless of what you may be learning from this breakup, chances are it will change your life. And that totally rocks!

FROM THE **breakup chronicles**

❝ On occasion, when I feel melancholy about oh-so-many short-term relationships, I mentally list things I learned to appreciate as a result of dating around: jazz, snowshoeing, hiking, Gilbert and Sullivan, art gallery openings, cowboy poetry, drumming, various musical artists, and (mmmmm) massage techniques. My life is richer and spicier thanks to the variety.**❞**

—*Jean*

Now, for the next few minutes think about what you might miss out on by never being *alone* for a significant amount of time in your adult life. Chances are, you know someone like that. She's floated from boyfriend to boyfriend, or worse, from husband to husband. While at one point or another you may have admired the fact that she's never without a date for the office party, that she always has someone to go on vacation with, and/or that she never sits home alone on a Saturday night, don't envy her.

If you happen to be one of these ladies, ask yourself this. If you flit from partner to partner, never truly being on your own, how do you know what makes *you* happy? How do you know what you have to offer someone else if you've never taken the time to discover it for yourself? There's nothing sexier than a woman who knows how to take care of herself, how to go after what she wants, and how to be happy on her own. That doesn't mean she can't be equally fabulous in a relationship—it just means that when she's in a relationship, she's even more fantastic because of the time she spent on her own, enjoying her own company and making her single life absolutely amazing.

Yes, some lucky ladies do get it right the first time around. They do marry young and stay happily married throughout their lives. And that's terrific! But it's rare. Chances are that if you're reading this book, that's not your particular path in life. (Let me remind you, that's a good thing.)

You've come this far. You've weathered the ups and downs of your Big Breakup. The worst is now behind you. What comes next is a breeze. In fact, I think you're going to find embracing your single self delightfully liberating (and fantastically fun!).

Beware of Dogs (and Dougs!)

Before we move on to Part Two, we have to have a little chat. Have you noticed that I haven't mentioned your ex lately? You've been doing so well I haven't felt the need to bring him up. But unfortunately, ex-boyfriends are notorious for knowing when you're about to dump your slump. It's like they installed a satellite to monitor your breakup recovery. While they've been courteous enough to leave you alone so far, now that you're ready to break up with your breakup, they may not be ready to let you. That satellite that's been watching you has just sounded an alarm bell, alerting Mr. Ex to your slump-dumping status.

RECOVERY R

In need of some pampering "me" time? Draw yourself a warm bath, pour in the bubbles, light some candles, and listen to Girl Power music while you soak away any residual breakup sadness.

Don't be surprised if your ex resurfaces at this point in time. And if he does, how are you going to handle it?

Exorcising Your Ex (One More Time!)

Chances are, you've fantasized about this moment ever since the breakup happened. The scenario in your head goes something like this:

Your ex shows up unannounced at your home/work/favorite hangout. He gets down on his knees and confesses all his horrible sins. Yes, he was a jerk. Yes, he treated you poorly. No, he didn't appreciate you, but now he does. Mr. Ex sheds a few tears (or sobs uncontrollably—it's your fantasy), blubbering on about what a huge mistake he made in losing you. His life has no meaning without you. He pleads with you to take pity on him and take him back.

At this point, what do you do?

1. You embrace him, tell him how much you've missed him, and the two of you lock in a passionate embrace (an obvious symbol of your *happily ever after* future together!).

2. You push him to the ground, drive your stiletto deep into his heart, and throw your head back, letting out an evil throaty laugh (proof positive that you are the breakup winner here!).

3. You smile compassionately and tell him that while you appreciate his honesty, the breakup has blessed

you with clarity, too. (And then you walk away with your head held high, knowing that in the end, you kept your cool without being cruel!)

Do any of these scenarios sound familiar? Or have you concocted something entirely different? In your fantasy, have you won the lottery? Found the man of your dreams, who just happens to be hotter/younger/wealthier/more successful than your ex? Have you lost twenty pounds and now look like a supermodel? Or do you have a big fat rock of an engagement ring on one hand, and a super sexy fiancé on the other? (If you're unsure or nervous about how you might handle a re-encounter with your ex, feel free to review the section on Ex Etiquette on page 15 in Chapter 1.)

Closing the Big Breakup Time Capsule

Ultimately, it doesn't matter whether or not your ex contacts you and/or tries to stop you from breaking up with your breakup. We both know you won't let him. We also know you won't go back to him (or take his *good-for-nothing* butt back!). You've come too far. And regardless of whether you're cautious, fiery, or fearless when it comes to dumping your slump, it's still time to retire those sweat pants (and any tear-stained T-shirts), not to mention your stock options in Kleenex and your subscription to *Woe Is Me Weekly*. It's also time to dig a hole in the backyard and gather any last-minute breakup bitterness along with those lingering revenge fantasies (*and* your rebound guy's phone number). Once you've put them in a time capsule—affectionately titled *My Big Breakup*—and buried them, I want you to observe a moment of silent gratitude for all that you've been through. Have you done all that? Good. Now it's time to go back inside, grab your Fabulous Factor list, sit in your most comfortable chair, and add at least three more things to the list, starting with *I just successfully broke up with my Big Breakup. I ROCK!*

And once again, I remind you . . .

Congratulations on your breakup!!!

And I ask you to join me this time.

Say it loud, say it proud . . .

"congratulations on your (my) breakup!!!"

You did it. You are a breakup recovery rock star! Your reward for all that hard work? You now get to throw yourself a movin' on party.

What are you waiting for?

It's time to move on to Part Two of this book.

end of part one *check-in*

Before we move on to Part Two, let's do one last check-in to assess your progress. Write down your five emotions here or in your journal. (Don't worry if you're still having some negative feelings. It doesn't mean you're not ready to move on. In fact, give yourself a pat on the back for your honesty. And if all your feelings are positive? That rocks, too!)

Now write down one thing you've learned so far about your breakup and/or breakup recovery. Make it just a sentence or two to encapsulate where you are right now. (For example, *"I realize now that I put too much of my energy and focus on my ex and not enough love and attention toward my own happiness. Never again!"*)

DATE [ ]

_____

_____

_____

_____

_____

_____

_____

Compare this list with your previous lists on pages 26, 47, 71, and 90. What's the most significant change you've noticed? The most difficult hurdle? What are you thinking about as you enter the next phase of your breakup recovery? What have you learned along the way?

107

part two
movin'ON

Wise Words from The Breakup Chronicles:

"It doesn't matter how many times you got hurt or got your heart broken for loving the wrong person or what you did in the past. What matters is you stood up from where you stumbled with your head up, and that you have moved on."

—*Ruby*

The Contract

In Part One, you put a lot of time and effort into dealing with and healing from your Big Breakup. In Part Two, your first order of business is to ensure that your hard work has not been in vain. How do we do that? By creating your very own accountability contract. The purpose of the contract is to acknowledge the pain of the past and to commit as much self-love and self-trust as possible to your future. Specifically, by signing the contract that follows (or creating one similar to it in your journal), you are agreeing to be the keeper of your heart. As the keeper of your heart, you promise to never give your love away foolishly and to be a wise judge of character when it comes to future relationships. This doesn't mean you can't date lots of different people while searching for a suitable long-term candidate (after all, variety is the single gal's spice of choice!). It just means that you now hold yourself accountable for your healed heart and all the work that went into its recovery, and that you promise to exercise excellent judgment when you're ready to fall in love again. (And in the meantime? Date away!)

Accountability Contract

You can read, sign, and date the contract here,

OR

You can rewrite the contract in your journal.

I, _____ , being of sound mind and healed heart, promise to be a worthy keeper of my healed heart. As the keeper of my healed heart, I agree to the following:

○ I will never again give my heart to anyone who is undeserving of it.

○ I will pay attention to relationship red flags as they are revealed to me and act accordingly.

○ When I'm ready, I trust myself to exercise excellent judgment in selecting a suitable candidate to fall in love with (one who is capable of loving me on the same level).

○ In the meantime, I trust myself to date (when I'm ready) and to be open to the possibilities.

○ I am healthy and strong enough to endure dating disappointments along the way, and I will be able to differentiate those disappointments from actual heartbreak.

○ I will not let any baggage from the past affect my future relationships. In fact, I have checked all unnecessary baggage and am now traveling with nothing more than a compact backpack full of lessons learned.

○ I dedicate myself wholeheartedly to living and loving my life as it is right now (and fixing the things that no longer work so I can live and love my life even more).

○ I recognize that having failed relationships in the past does not make me a failure at love.

○ I am now free to welcome (at my discretion) healthy, happy, whole love into my life!

Signed: _____ Date: _____

Congratulations! Your heart is now in excellent hands.

> WHAT YOU SAID: "I just don't know how I'll live without you."

> WHAT YOU MEANT: "I'm not sure how I'll live without you, but I'm sure gonna have fun trying!"

CHAPTER SIX
you're INVITED

Welcome to the beginning of the rest of your amazing life, also known as Movin' On mode. Whether you know it or not, by going through the pain of your Big Breakup and giving yourself permission to move on, you have greatly increased your odds of living *happily ever after*. Isn't that fantastic?!

Now that you're in Movin' On mode, your first mission, should you choose to accept it (and you really should) is to throw yourself a Movin' On party. Chances are that you've never been to a Movin' On party before. And that's okay! In fact, it's to be expected. While we've all been to parties for soon-to-be newlyweds, gift-giving gatherings when vows are exchanged, and celebrations for babies-to-be, in the past there was no similar formal occasion to commemorate when someone moved on from her Big Breakup. That's all about to change because just as engagements and weddings and babies count as life-altering events, so too does walking away from the wrong relationship and movin' on to a life better suited for you. In choosing you—*amazing you*—over a relationship that wasn't working and a breakup that needed to be broken up with, you've proven just how incredibly brave and bold you are. And I think that's definitely something worth celebrating. (In other words, let the Movin' On party begin!)

RECOVERY

In need of some serious snuggle time while you plan your Movin' On party? Ask a friend if you can borrow her dog for a day. Go for a walk, play in the park, and take a snuggle nap together. Or volunteer for a day at your local animal shelter. Play with the puppies, cuddle with the cats, and just have fun. (The love and affection of animals does the soul good!)

Not exactly a party-planning aficionado? Fear not! If you look back at my Fabulous Factor list on page 69, you'll notice that I happen to be a seasoned pro at throwing a killer party. So you're in very capable hands. When in doubt, you can always ask a friend to cohost your party. In fact, before we proceed any further into Part Two, we need to first give props to your Boo-Hoo Crew. See, you're not the only one who's moved on. Your Boo-Hoo Crew has racked up enough post-breakup brownie points for a serious celebration. To thank them for their tireless service in your time of need, you may now promote your Boo-Hoo Crew to your Woo-Hoo Crew.

Your what?

Your Woo-Hoo Crew, also known as your incredibly loyal friends who are now free to celebrate your single status along with you. They got you through the hard times—now it's time to have some fun. So call up the girls and let them know that the mourning period has ended. It's now time to throw your Movin' On party!

Party Planning 101

Now that your Woo-Hoo Crew is on board, let's determine what kind of Movin' On party you want to throw.

What kind of party do you envision?

○ Low-key/mellow
○ Fun and fab
○ Wild and crazy

Who will you invite?

○ Your inner circle
○ Your close friends and a few favorite acquaintances
○ Everyone you know

What do you see people doing?

○ Dining in style
○ Mingling and talking
○ Dancing the night away

What kind of hostess do you want to be?

○ The hostess with the mostess
○ Single and ready to mingle
○ The life of the party

Once you've answered these questions, you'll most likely have the kind of party you want to throw in mind. And chances are, it will be one of the following:

○ A dinner party
○ A cocktail party
○ A night out dancing with the girls
○ Some variation of the above

After you've decided on the type of celebratory shindig you want to throw, it's time to put your plans in motion. Remember, this party is all about celebrating *you,* so it should be your idea of a good time, whatever form that takes. From the location to the guest list to the activities and the menu—you get to call the shots (oooh, shots!).

Location

Now we address the issue of where to hold your soirée. Unless you're opposed to the idea, I suggest hosting it at your place (home field advantage is a definite *plus*!). The benefits of a home-based party include the following:

1. You're probably comfortable playing hostess there.
2. You get to christen your post-breakup space with the help of your fabulous friends' love and energy.
3. You don't have to think about a designated driver if you get a little tipsy.

If, on the other hand, your place isn't party-friendly for one reason or another, you can always host your party at a friend's house (maybe someone from your Woo-Hoo Crew), a favorite bar or restaurant, or some other party-friendly location. If it's a public place, just be sure to choose somewhere you love that doesn't in any way remind you of your ex or pose the possibility that your ex might show up. After all, this is your Movin' On party—no exes allowed!

The Guest List

Next, it's time to create the guest list (and check it twice!). Who you invite depends on the type of party you're throwing and the amount of space you have. If you're having a sit-down dinner party, for example, your guest list will be smaller than if you're having a standing-and-mingling cocktail party. And if you're going out dancing with the girls, well, that has some influence on your choice of invitees, too.

Ultimately, when planning your Movin' On party, it's important to remember that it's your soiree and the guest list is completely up to you. You can invite whomever you want and specifically *not* invite anyone you don't want. Not sure about those fringe friends who have your ex's number on speed dial and would most likely report every party detail back to him? Or that well-meaning but gossipy coworker who will no doubt dish about your every Movin' On move the next morning on her blog or MySpace page? Save yourself the hassle and nix them from the invite list. It's not every day you throw a Movin' On party. This is one of the few times in life that you get to be selfish. So give yourself permission to include only those friends who are supportive of this transitional time in your life and are worthy of celebrating with you.

The following are guest list considerations for each type of party.

The Dinner Party

The most successful dinner parties feature great food, lively conversation, and the right location. Once you've determined if your guests are dining at your table or someone else's, you'll next want to select the perfect cast of characters to join your celebratory soiree. Of course your Woo-Hoo Crew and other close friends are a shoo-in for an invite, but what about that fun new acquaintance who tells the best stories, or your fringe friend who's always up on the latest current events? Inviting a few new guests to the dinner table could add just the right amount of spice to your evening. Plus, it's fun to mix old and new friends. After all, this is your Movin' On party—feel free to shake things up. (You never know what'll happen!)

The Cocktail Party

The recipe for a successful cocktail party goes something like this: one part eclectic guest list, two parts delicious drinks, a splash of mood music, and the perfect hostess to shake it all up. And if you're single and ready to mingle? Then a cocktail party is a must for your Movin' On party. It not only allows you to invite all of your friends and acquaintances, but it also allows them to invite their friends as well. This increases the odds of meeting someone new. Even if you're not ready to date yet, it's fun to get your flirt on for a night. If nothing else, it's good practice for when you *are* ready to start dating again. And it can be a real ego boost if you happen to meet a cute party crasher who finds you irresistible!

Cocktail parties are the most fun when you've got a decent male-to-female ratio and not everyone knows each other. This allows for the element of surprise, refreshingly bold conversations, and even a possible hookup or two. Even if you're not the one hooking up, being the hookup hostess earns you more than a few cool points.

Dancing with the Girls

For some fun-loving females, the perfect Movin' On party is a night out dancing with their girlfriends. After all, what better way to shake things up than by shaking your groove thang? If this is the Movin' On party for you, then you first need to figure out where you're gonna get your groove on. If you plan on flirting with fine-looking fellas, then do your research on where the hottest new club is near where you live. Or, if you're just looking to have some fun with your g.f.'s, you may want to hit one of the gay clubs. Oftentimes, the music's better, the guys are cuter (and a lot more fun to talk to), *plus* you don't have to worry about getting hit on.

Not long after my Big Breakup, I went out dancing at a gay club with a group of g.f.'s and it was just the antidote I needed to cure my breakup blues. The deejay was hot, the boys were super cute, and the male-to-female ratio was just right for my first night out as a newly single gal. If what you really want is to shake things up at your Movin' On party, then it's time to gather the girls and dance the night away!

The Menu

Once you've created the guest list, it's time to work on the menu. And because the menu also depends on the type of party you're throwing, the following are some suggestions and considerations when planning your movin' on menu.

The Dinner Party

Hosting a dinner party can be tons of fun—and a lot of work! Fortunately, you have plenty of options to help make the evening easier on you. If you're not so handy in the kitchen or short on serving dishes, host a potluck and ask each of your guests to bring a dish. Or if most of your guests are equally culinarily challenged, you can opt to cater the event from your favorite restaurant (all the fun and convenience of eating out with the coziness and privacy of eating in). Or if you're a whiz in the kitchen, you can create the entire meal from scratch. Of course, I recommend having a helper or two in the kitchen—feeding your friends is no easy feat!

POTLUCK PARTY TIP

To ensure you've got a well-rounded meal of appetizers, main dish, side dishes, drinks, and dessert, you may want to ask guests to sign up for what they're bringing in advance. Or create a dinner party theme or ethnic food fest and make suggestions for what you'd like guests to bring.

Next, you'll want to find out if any of your guests have dietary restrictions. Are they vegetarian? Vegan? Does anyone have food allergies? These answers will help shape the evening's menu (and save you the hassle and embarrassment of serving pot roast to a bunch of non-meat eaters!).

TIPS FOR FEEDING FINICKY FRIENDS

While hosting a dinner party can be fun, it can also prove a bit challenging if your guests have dietary restrictions. But fear not, my fab friend. The following are some tips for dealing with picky dinner party guests:

- Host a fondue party where everyone brings a sauce or dipping-friendly finger food. That way, each and every guest is bringing something to the party that they can actually eat!
- Ask your vegan and vegetarian friends to each bring a favorite dish that they'd be willing to share with other party guests.
- Because everyone has different dietary wants and needs, serve all sauces and dressings on the side.
- Finally, accept that you're not Wonder Woman and ask for help both in the kitchen and with party planning as needed!

Now that you've got your finicky eaters figured out, the following are some additional party planning considerations to ponder:

○ What kind of pre-dinner snacks/appetizers will you serve?
○ What type of pre-dinner activities do you have planned?
○ What beverages will you have on hand (both alcoholic and nonalcoholic)?
○ What dessert will complement the meal?
○ What after-dinner activities do you have planned?

Some of your guests may arrive before dinner is served (maybe even while you're still preparing the meal), which means you need to have some activities planned to keep them entertained. The following are some suggested ways to entertain your guests before sitting down to dinner:

○ Invite your early arriving friend(s) to get the party started by picking the first few CDs your guests will listen to.
○ Ask your early arrivers if they'll help you set the table, then once everyone sits down to dinner, acknowledge their efforts.
○ Invite one of your friends to answer the front door. That way, you can concentrate on finishing up any last-minute meal prep as guests continue to arrive.
○ Encourage an early bird to act as bartender and open a bottle of wine or champagne. Then have a private toast with your prompt friends to kick-start the revelry.

And to keep the party going long after dinner's been served, try one or more of the following activities (see the following page):

○ Ask your friends to bring their favorite board games. After dinner, take a vote on which one to play first. Cranium, Balderdash, and Catch Phrase are great group games. (And of course charades, Twister, and strip poker are tons of retro fun, too!)

○ Make dessert a group activity by asking everyone to bring an ingredient for ice cream sundaes. Let everyone concoct their favorite and then pass them around.

○ After dessert, head to your local dive bar for drinks and darts. (If you happen to meet a cutie or two, you'll have plenty of wing men and women to help with a hookup!)

○ Break out one of those murder mystery games and play until the murderer is found.

○ Rent some movies and let guests vote on which one to watch first.

○ If you've got access to a hot tub or Jacuzzi, invite guests to bring their bathing suits and go for a post-dinner soak (talk about heating things up!).

BEFORE-PARTY INVENTORY

As you make plans for your dinner party, you'll also want to take stock of your kitchen to see if you have everything you need to serve your guests. Do you have enough plates? Wine glasses? Serving bowls and utensils? A nice tablecloth? If not, splurge a little on acquiring these new things for yourself. Or, if you're on a budget, ask to borrow from friends or have fun mixing and matching unique items from thrift, secondhand, and consignment shops. Or, if most of your kitchen items happened to belong to your ex and you don't have the time, money, or inclination to restock before your shindig, you can throw a Disposable Dinner Party using paper and plastic products. (This dinner party is especially fun if you ask your guests to dress up!) And here's another idea. Just like friends register for bridal showers, weddings, and baby showers, you too deserve to register for this life-changing occasion. Why not create a Movin' On wish list of all the things you need at your favorite online store? Register ahead of time and then recruit your Woo-Hoo Crew to spread the word, encouraging guests to bring your gifts to the party where you can unwrap and use them.

Point, Click, Shop!

Stumped for where to register? Create your Movin' On wish list at any of the following online retailers:

○ *Target.com* (everything you need under one roof)
○ *Overstock.com* (great deals on anything and everything you can imagine)
○ *PotteryBarn.com* (furnish any room in your home with style)
○ *WorldMarket.com* (whether you're dreaming of new dishes, stylish serving ware, or eclectic accessories, Cost Plus World Market has it all)
○ *Williams-Sonoma.com* (for you high-end kitchen appliance and gadget lovers)

Of course, feel free to pick your own favorite shopping site, too!

The Cocktail Party

If you're hosting a cocktail party, your menu will be a little different. You probably won't be serving a full meal, but you will want to have plenty of snacks and appetizers on hand (and ones that go well with your cocktail menu, i.e. chips and guacamole with margaritas, brie and crackers with wine, and so on.). As for the drink menu, ask your friends to bring ingredients for their favorite beverages. You may also want to consider coming up with a signature drink for the evening. Like a Movin' On Martini or Back in the Saddle Punch. There are plenty of bartending books out there and online resources to help you concoct your cocktail menu. In the meantime, the following are a few fun drinks to try.

"GET YOUR FLIRT ON" FLIRTINI

Just a sip or two of this light and refreshing cocktail will have you and your guests feeling flirty (and possibly frisky) in no time!

½ oz Cointreau orange liqueur
½ oz vodka
2 oz pineapple juice
3 oz champagne
Maraschino cherries

1. Combine pineapple juice, Cointreau, and vodka in a shaker with ice.
2. Strain into a chilled cocktail glass and top with champagne.
3. Garnish with a cherry and serve. (Yum!)

"MOVIN' ON" CHOCOLATE MARTINI

This sweet concoction is sure to be the hit of the party (and to help you and your partygoers get your Movin' On groove on!).

1½ oz Stoli Vanilla vodka
1 oz Godiva chocolate liqueur
Maraschino cherries

1. Mix vanilla vodka and chocolate liqueur in a shaker filled with ice.
2. Strain into either chilled wine or martini glasses. Garnish with a cherry. (Sinfully sweet!)

"SINGLE & READY TO MINGLE" CARAMEL APPLE MARTINI

This sweet-with-a-kick cocktail will kick-start your Movin' On party into serious celebration mode!

2 oz Bacardi Big Apple rum
2 oz butterscotch schnapps
Thin slices of red apple

1. Combine schnapps and rum in a cocktail shaker with ice.
2. Shake well and then strain into 2 chilled martini glasses.
3. Garnish with a red apple wedge and serve. (Decadent and delish!)

Unsure of your martini mixing skills? If you're a bartending novice, ask around. You most likely have a friend or two who would love to play bartender for a night. Then again, it wouldn't hurt to brush up on your own bartending skills. Think about all the people you'll connect with if you're in charge of drinks—not only old friends but potentially some cute new acquaintances, too. (I'll drink to that!)

When it comes to dressing for a cocktail party, pretty much anything goes. However, you may want to set a dress code, asking guests to wear their party best or dress up according to your party theme (a Roaring Twenties gangster-and-flapper theme, a pirate booty blowout, safari chic, or a 1960s free-love fest).

And depending on how well your guests know each other, you may want to introduce some icebreaker games to help set the mood for your cocktail party. The following are a few suggested activities:

○ On index cards, write down the names of famous/influential figures throughout history and as your guests arrive, tape one name to the back of each guest. Invite your friends to make conversation with one another based on the name on their back (of course, they cannot use the person's actual name or the name of their spouse or significant other). This game is the most fun when you have controversial figures like Michael Jackson, Paris Hilton, and Simon Cowell whom everyone knows and most likely has strong and/or funny opinions about.

○ Invite each guest to write down one little-known fact/secret about themselves on a scrap of paper. Fold each one and put them in a hat or jar. Ask each guest to draw one secret out. Guests must then circulate during the party asking questions of everyone until they find the person whose fact or secret they have. If guests are stumped for ideas, encourage them to write down something from their childhood or college days that most people probably don't know about them (for example, *I was my high school mascot* or *My first teenage crush was David Cassidy*).

○ Break out a DVD trivia game and invite guests to play.

COCKTAIL PARTY MENU TIPS

If you're having a cocktail party, you'll want to plan your menu keeping in mind that people will be standing and mingling (rather than sitting down with plates, utensils, and napkins in their laps). Therefore, the following do's and don'ts should be adhered to:

Do Feature fun finger foods like cheese and crackers, stuffed mushrooms, skewered chicken satay, and other bite-size appetizers.

Don't Include messy, goopy, accident-friendly foods like huge slices of pizza, chili, or pasta (nothing says *Party foul!* quite like marinara sauce on the carpet or couch).

Dancing with the Girls

If you're planning on going out dancing with your g.f.'s, your menu will probably be secondary to where you're going and what you're wearing. Still, you could host pre-dancing cocktails at your place to kick the night off, or have the girls bring their sleeping bags over and host a post-dancing slumber party complete with late-night munchies brought on by burning all those dancing calories. (FYI—you can cook S'mores in the microwave or on your gas stove. Just a snack suggestion every savvy single gal should know about!)

Not sure what to wear on your Girls' Night Out? The following are some do's and don'ts that should help.

Wardrobe Tips

○ Do wear something that makes you feel good about yourself. (Believe it or not, you'll be a better dancer if you're feeling cute.)
○ Do wear comfortable shoes. (Your feet will thank you.)
○ Do wear something conducive to lots of movement (nothing too tight or too loose).
○ Don't wear anything that runs the risk of ripping, falling off, or causing a body part to pop out. (Can you say *wardrobe malfunction*?!)

○ Don't choose style over comfort. (A fabulous outfit only works if you're not grimacing or constantly readjusting the whole night.)

○ Don't go bra-less. (Your boobs will thank you the next day!) And don't forget your underwear!

Invitations, Ambience, and Other Party-Planning Tips

Depending on your personality, party planning can either be fun or fearsome. If you're feeling overwhelmed or out of your league, you can always ask a friend for help. When in doubt, making a list (or lists) will help you stay organized. After all, the purpose of this party isn't to make you tear your hair out or send you retreating under the covers until your Woo-Hoo Crew stages an intervention. The goal here is to celebrate you and your new life as a savvy single gal who's no longer coupled up with what's-his-name. Make things as easy as possible so that you can just enjoy what's to come. With this mantra in mind, the following smaller details should help round out your party plans.

The Invitations

Once you've finalized the guest list, it's time to create and send your Movin' On party invitations. *Evite.com* is perfect for this type of occasion. It's less formal (and less expensive) than sending traditional invitations through the mail, and it's more personal than sending out a mass e-mail or making tons of calls to voicemail boxes and answering machines.

Before sending out your invitations, here's something important to consider—do you want everyone to know the purpose of this party, or would you rather they just thought of it as yet another fun get-together among friends? It's up to you how much you want to tout this shindig as your Movin' On party. You may want to be loud and proud about your party theme, or you may want to keep it on the down low. Or you can recruit your Woo-Hoo Crew to shout it from the rooftops if you don't quite feel comfortable doing so yourself. The way you choose to promote your party is entirely up to you (and should match your comfort level).

YOU'VE GOT MAIL!

Want to send personalized invitations announcing your Movin' On party? My breakup shop at *www.cafepress.com/breakupshop* features an eclectic selection of greeting and meeting cards tailored to announcing breakups, celebrating your single status, and letting people know that you're *single and ready to mingle* (and that they're invited to the party!).

The ABCs of Ambience

When it comes to your Movin' On party's ambience, much of that will once again depend on the type of party you're throwing. A nicely set table, soft music, and the heavenly smells of a lip-smacking meal will help set the tone for your dinner party. In the same way, some eclectic lounge music, candles, and other mood lighting will create just the right vibe for your cocktail party, along with fun cocktail napkins, a fully stocked bar, and finger foods strategically placed throughout your home. And a late-afternoon mani-pedi session with the girls will most likely get that dance party started on the right foot (complete with pretty painted toes!).

Regardless of what type of party you're throwing, here's another celebration suggestion. Buy a bunch of disposable cameras and place them throughout your home. Encourage your guests to take random photos throughout the party. You can do the same with a digital camera, but there's something fun about giving your guests creative license to capture moments on their own that you'll later enjoy reliving once you've developed the film. (Better yet, ask the photo lab for a CD of your party prints so you can upload and share your party photo album with friends!) Not only will you want visual memories of your Movin' On party, but you may want musical ones as well.

EX-BOYFRIEND ALERT

Through the grapevine, your ex may get wind of your Movin' On party. Whether he calls, e-mails, or grills a friend of a friend for the inside scoop, the answer's always the same—*None of your business.* (You can tell him so right before you hang up the phone.) Be strong. Keep your boundaries firmly intact. And then pat yourself on the back for being such a breakup recovery rock star!

Here are a few suggestions for creating a soundtrack to your party:

○ Ask your friends to each bring a favorite party CD or iPod mix and then shuffle the music on your CD player, computer, or iPod.
○ Create your very own Movin' On mix ahead of time from your personal music collection or by downloading music online. (You could even make copies and pass out your mix to guests as a party favor.)
○ If you have a friend who loves to mix music, ask her to deejay your Movin' On party. (That oughtta impress your guests!)

Party Prep

Once your party plans are finalized, you'll want to make a shopping list of everything you need. I suggest doing your shopping ahead of time so you're not stressed out come party time. You can always make a last-minute run to the grocery store, but you'll be much more relaxed at your party if you do your prep work with time to spare. The following is a pre-party shopping list cheat sheet that should help get you ready for the big day. Feel free to fill in the details on your own shopping list for each of the items listed below.

Pre-Party Shopping List

○ Food (appetizers, snacks, main course, side dishes, dessert)
○ Drinks (alcoholic and nonalcoholic) and glasses
○ Ice (you don't want to run out)
○ Serving ware, utensils, etc. (ask to borrow from friends if you need to)
○ Cocktail napkins and other linens
○ Party favors (disposable cameras, CDs, etc.)

On a budget? Before you go shopping, you'll want to identify how much you're comfortable spending on your party. If you don't think your budget will cover everything you need, call up your Woo-Hoo Crew and ask them to each bring an item or two from your list. While planning and hosting a party takes time, energy, and money, the most important thing to remember is this. You don't have to break the bank to throw a memorable Movin' On party. In the end, it's not how much you spend but how much you celebrate that makes your party a success!

Mirror, Mirror on the Wall

Don't think I forgot the most important detail of your celebratory shindig. I was just saving the best for last. Now it's time to talk about your Movin' On party outfit. Do a quick mental walkthrough of your closet. Anything come to mind that's party perfect? Since the purpose of this celebration is to show how far you've come since your Big Breakup, you should wear something that makes you feel amazing. If your closet's looking a little drab, then you gotta go shopping!

A shopping spree the weekend before your party will give you plenty of time to pick and choose the perfect party ensemble. That way you're not pressed for time and can find just the right outfit and accessories. If you're not sure what to wear, or if shopping's not really your thing, invite someone from your Woo-Hoo Crew along who knows your style and can help you find just the right look for your big party.

On a budget? Add some sass to your existing wardrobe with a new pair of shoes or some fabulously fun accessories, or update your hairstyle with a cut, color, and highlights. If you're *really* trying to cut costs, you can always ask to borrow something from a friend's wardrobe. It doesn't have to be new—maybe just new to you!

Last-Minute Details

In the week leading up to your party, you'll want to take a look around your home to see if it's party-friendly. Are there plenty of places to sit? Is there enough mingling room? Do you need to move furniture around to make way for your Movin' On party? Or do you need to borrow some chairs from a friend? And most importantly, has all evidence of your ex been extracted? I know we did a thorough exorcism in Part One, but there may be an item or two you've been holding onto until now. Like that photo collage on the wall that just happens to have a picture or two of you and your ex in happier times. Or the universal remote that you held onto in your post-breakup rage, even though it no longer controls any electronics now that he's out of the picture. If you've got any lingering ex accessories lying around, now's the time to let them go. Toss it, torch it, donate it, or dump it—*now*. (Good job!) Once you've removed any remaining ex-related items, made any last-minute menu tweaks, and given your home a thorough pre-party cleaning, your place should be party perfect (and dust-free).

Party Time, Excellent!

When the big day arrives, you should wake up feeling well rested and perfectly prepared. To kick-start the celebration, why not treat yourself to a relaxing massage and/or mani-pedi at your favorite spa early in the day? It's the perfect way to ensure that you'll be refreshed, relaxed, and ready to celebrate come party time. You'll want to give yourself plenty of time to shower, get dressed, and do your hair and makeup. This is one day when you should not feel rushed in any way. You can even treat yourself to a pre-party cocktail at home while putting the finishing touches on your face or setting up for the party. And if you need any last-minute help, invite your Woo-Hoo Crew to join you for that pre-party cocktail and any final party prep.

Once the guests start arriving, it's time for you to relax, smile, and enjoy. Remember, this party is all about celebrating you and your amazing recovery. It's just the beginning of your Movin' On journey, so let the party begin!

CHANNELING YOUR INNER HOSTESS WITH THE MOSTESS

If this is your first party flying solo in a long time, don't stress. You don't have to have a man on your arm to have a good time. Give yourself permission to be your own arm candy. Circulate, smile, laugh, flirt, get your buzz on. This is just the beginning of you rediscovering your fabulous single self. (So go ahead—work it, girl!)

As you circulate among your party guests, think about this. You never know who you might be inspiring right now. By being such a brave and bold breakup survivor (and a terrific party hostess), you may just be showing one or more of your fab friends that while breaking up can be hard, ending a relationship with the wrong person is always the right thing to do. Even if you got broken up with, your survival skills are probably inspiring someone who's contemplating a breakup right this very minute. Not only has your breakup changed your life, but it just might be changing someone else's, too. (Isn't that cool?!)

between-chapter *check-in*

In Part Two, your check-ins are going to be a little different. We'll still be gauging where you are emotionally, but the check-in will be tailored to the subject of the chapter you just finished. Here or in your journal, write down a highlight or two from your Movin' On party. If you haven't thrown your party yet, be sure to return to this page once you have. While it may not seem like it, your Movin' On party is instrumental to your progress in Part Two. It's important to acknowledge and celebrate your breakup recovery and all the lessons you've learned along the way. So take a minute to reflect and write about a party highlight either below or in your journal.

Example: *I was surprised by some of the people who showed up to my Movin' On party, and how supportive my friends were of my breakup recovery. (And btw, I also discovered that I make a mean Movin' On Chocolate Martini!)*

DATE [   ] _____

_____

_____

_____

_____

CHAPTER SEVEN

getting back
to the business of YOU

as you ease into Movin' On mode, you may find that just as you did during your initial post-breakup timeline, you have good days and bad ones. There will be times when you leap forward, embracing the pleasures that come with living life on your own terms, discovering new and fabulous ways to occupy your time, and applying those hard-earned breakup lessons. And then there may be days when it feels like you've taken a U-turn in your recovery, and all you want to do is hide under the covers curled up in the fetal position.

Guess what? You're doing everything right. You *are* making progress. Like a caterpillar that creates a cocoon, hibernates, and eventually emerges as a beautiful butterfly, you too are transforming yourself and your life. And that takes patience and time. Whether you're still feeling like that caterpillar, inching along in your post-breakup recovery; are comfortably nestled in your recovery cocoon while you lick your wounds and continue to heal; or are ready to break free and fly like the brave and bold butterfly you are remains to be seen (and probably depends on the day).

> ## movin' on secret #1
> Just because you're in Movin' On mode doesn't mean you won't still feel vulnerable, sad, or a little bit confused from time to time about your breakup. Your recovery will most likely extend well into Part Two of this book. And that's perfectly normal.

Of course, if you're feeling like your old self again and your breakup is nothing but a distant memory, that's normal, too. And if you're somewhere in the middle—maybe you're content staying in every night of the week and weekend watching movies without any interest in putting yourself out there yet, well that's just fine, too. You're entitled to enjoy the warmth and safety of your cocoon for as long as you want. But guess what? You will eventually become that breathtaking butterfly. It's just a matter of time until you're ready to spread your wings and fly.

In order to get there, let's first determine where you are in your Movin' On metamorphosis. Then we'll know how to get back to the business of you—who you were before the breakup, who you are now, and who you want to become as a result of all the juicy life lessons you've learned (and continue to learn) along the road to recovery.

De-Mystifying Movin' On Mode
Now it's time to figure out what being in each particular mode means to your Movin' On recovery.

Movin' On Metamorphosis Quiz

Which of the following best describes your typical first thought when you wake up in the morning?

1. "I wonder what my ex is doing. Does he miss me?"
2. "I can't believe I'm single again. Better hit the snooze button."
3. "Today's gonna be a busy day. Time to hop to it!"

Which of the following best describes your typical last thought before you go to sleep at night?

1. "I wonder *who* my ex is doing."
2. "Did I really eat all the ice cream again?"
3. "I'm so glad what's-his-name is no longer here to hog all the covers."

A member of your Woo-Hoo Crew has invited you to a party. Which best describes your reaction?

1. "I don't know if I can go. What if *he's* there?"
2. "If we're gonna do girls' night, couldn't we just stay home and have fun?"
3. "I can't wait—*everyone's* gonna be there!"

And finally . . . while waiting in line for coffee, the cutie in front of you strikes up a conversation. After paying for his latte, he asks for your number. You:

1. Chase him away with your flustered reaction.
2. Blush, smile, and tell him you that while you're flattered, you're just not into dating right now.
3. Flash your pearly whites and give him your number, thinking *Why not?*

Movin' On Metamorphosis Quiz scoring

Scoring: By now, you're probably getting the picture. If you mostly answered 1, you're still in caterpillar mode. If you chose mostly 2s, you're in serious cocoon mode. And if most of your answers were 3, well *hallelujah*, you're ready to bust out and be that breathtaking butterfly!

Caterpillar Mode

The beauty of being in caterpillar mode is that there's so much to look forward to. Yes, you may be movin' on at a snail's pace, but even snails reach their destination eventually. And they have plenty of time to enjoy the horizon ahead of them. (So do you!) While taking your sweet time in adjusting to your new life and its endless possibilities can be good, you'll want to make sure you're not hindering your recovery by moving too slowly. Yes, change is hard. But so is holding onto a life that no longer works for you.

Let me remind you that *surviving* your breakup was the hard part. Now all you have to do is be open to a life better suited for you. A life you deserve to love. A life that doesn't include an ex who wasn't right for you and that *can* include someone amazing when you're ready to fall in love again. Remember, you're the keeper of your heart. Only you will know when you're ready to fall in love, and then it's up to you to filter out the unworthy candidates until you find a suitable match who's as healthy, happy, and as whole as you are.

If you find yourself still in caterpillar mode, don't worry. You're still making progress. And in hopes of kick-starting that progress, I've got an exercise just for you. Get out your journal and write down the name of someone you admire. It can be someone you know (a friend, relative, coworker, or mentor) or someone you don't (someone in the public eye or an influential figure in history). What's important here is to choose someone who you think lives (or lived) her life in ways you admire. Maybe she's a risk taker. Maybe she live(d) her life with authenticity and purpose. Or maybe she's been successful at something you'd like to one day succeed at. (If you think of more than one person, go ahead and write down as many people as you like.)

Next, write down at least five things that you admire about each person on your list. Don't rush this exercise. Really take your time to identify the traits and qualities you genuinely admire about each person. Once you've done that, I want you to look back at the list and reflect on how you could start embodying some of those admirable traits. Right here and now, what could you do to not only celebrate that person you admire, but to celebrate yourself, too?

It's time to start thinking of yourself as the heroine of your own life. You've already been incredibly brave and bold in your breakup recovery. It's time to acknowledge just how amazing you are and get your Movin' On groove on!

The following is my list of people I admire. Feel free to borrow from or be inspired by it.

Lisa's List: Heroines I Admire

Tina Turner: While there are lots of reasons to admire Ms. Turner, the following are my top five.

1. She overcame incredibly difficult circumstances (poverty, abusive relationship) to become one of the world's most successful singers of all time.
2. She exudes beauty, grace, class, and poise.
3. She's had an amazing career (longevity rocks!).
4. She makes 60-plus look amazing (those legs!).
5. She can *sing* (that voice!).

I especially admire Tina Turner's inner strength. It must have taken so much courage to walk away from the fame and the controlling relationship she had with Ike Turner and start all over again. I admire her resilience and hope to embody these admirable traits as I continue in Movin' On mode.

Angelina Jolie: Say what you will about Brangelina, but on her own Ms. Jolie has done a world of good for so many people. (And I think this book is big enough to give props to both Jen *and* Angie!) So retire your *Team Aniston* or *Team Jolie* T-shirts and join forces to see why I think Angelina rocks.

1. She uses her fame for good (UN ambassador, pro-adoption, gives one-third of her income to charity).
2. She's unapologetic about how she lives her life.
3. She puts her kids first.
4. She never lets a man rule her life. (Anyone besides me think Brad might be a little bit whipped?)
5. She goes after what she wants with passion and determination.

Angelina exudes passion, drive, and determination, all traits I'd love to embody. Plus, she seems to have grown a lot from her Billy Bob days. I hope to emerge from my post-breakup cocoon and become a beautiful butterfly like she has.

Hilary Clinton: You don't have to agree with her politics *or* her personal life to acknowledge that this former first lady rocks for the following reasons.

1. She is unapologetic in her beliefs.
2. She's made a name and career for herself rather than riding on her husband's coattails.

3. She defines what it means to be a strong woman.

4. She doesn't crumble when faced with challenges or adversity.

5. She seems passionate about making a difference in the world.

I admire Hilary's incredible strength and her ability to stand up for what she believes in with the courage of her convictions. I hope to be as strong and steadfast in my own life with my own passionate beliefs.

Now it's your turn. Who do you admire? (If you haven't already, make your list!)

Becoming the Heroine of Your Own Life

Regardless of where you are in your Movin' On metamorphosis, the following are some ways you can become more courageous, strong, and downright Wonder Woman–like in your everyday existence.

VOLUNTEER YOUR TIME

Why not devote some of that fabulous Movin' On energy to a volunteer project in your community or a cause near and dear to your heart? Even if you don't have a particular cause in mind, there are plenty of volunteer organizations that could use your help. The Boys And Girls Club of America; a local shelter for the homeless, battered women, or animals; or a community project in your city or town are all possible places to start. Doing something good for others, even if it's just one Saturday a month, can make a world of difference in both your life and the lives of those you help.

And in case you need reminding, you never know who you'll meet *or* who you'll inspire!

FACE A FEAR

As daunting as it may seem at first, facing a fear can be incredibly liberating. You'll definitely become the heroine of your own life if you enroll in that public speaking class or Toastmasters Club; learn how to swim after all these years; or approach and talk to that cute stranger you always see but have never had the guts to talk to before at the grocery store/laundromat/coffee cart outside your office building. (Go for it!)

FOLLOW A DREAM

Is there a secret burning desire lurking just below the surface of your everyday existence? Have you:

- ○ Always wanted to take an improv class?
- ○ Been secretly writing poetry for years without anyone knowing it?
- ○ Gone to bed most nights thinking about swimming with dolphins?
- ○ Dreamt about skydiving out of an airplane but never had the guts to go for it?

What's stopping you from following that dream you've harbored for far too long? Fear? Forget it! Practicality? Throw caution to the wind for a change! As the heroine of your own life, you're now free to try daring feats. Take risks. Stare death in the face and laugh. Or at least make an effort to pursue that passion that keeps you awake nights.

> *movin' on secret #2*
> You don't have to quit your day job to become more heroic.

LIFE LESSONS 101

In case nobody ever told you, you only live once. And as cheesy as those bumper stickers are, they're right—life is *not* a dress rehearsal. So gather some gumption and embody that heroine you've only dared to dream about becoming. This is your life—you deserve to live it up!

Why not take that fabulous vacation where you snorkel, suntan, and swim with the dolphins; or join an improv troupe in your spare time and just have fun; enter a poetry contest; or even locate your local skydiving hangar and take a tandem jump to whet your appetite for adventure (and possibly sign up for lessons so you can learn how to jump on your own)?

Cocoon Mode

If you're in cocoon mode, I have to admit I'm so excited for you! After my Big Breakup, one of the best things I ever did was allow myself plenty of cocoon time. Before that breakup, I'd always considered myself a better friend to others than to myself. I flitted from one friend to another, and sometimes one boyfriend to another, always paying more attention to other people's needs than my own. When I finally ended things for good with Mr. Ex, I was exhausted and a mess. After enduring a very long and painful breakup recovery (prolonged by my own unwillingness to let go and get on with things), I finally graduated to Movin' On mode. I bought my first home, a cute condo that I enjoyed fixing up and decorating (in a neighborhood Mr. Ex would have hated but that I loved). Whereas once upon a time staying home on a Friday night would have felt like the kiss of death, I began to revel in my alone time, preferring the company of myself and my cats to even the *thought* of embarking on a blind date or hitting the bar scene to scope out someone new with my Woo-Hoo Crew. At first, my friends were confused. Why was I suddenly turning down dinner invitations and flaking on group gatherings? In time, they came to understand that I was just content in cocoon mode. I would come out of it eventually but for the time being it was exactly what I needed.

Chances are that hunkering down in your own cocoon is exactly what you need, too. Taking time for yourself, your healing, and for really figuring out what you want to do with the rest of your life is so important. That's what cocoon mode is all about. Don't beat yourself up or get impatient with your progress. Just enjoy being a little self-indulgent. When you're ready, you'll emerge as the incredible butterfly we both know that you are. And you'll be better prepared to take on the world because you first took care of yourself.

THE JOYS OF COCOON MODE

Loving every minute of your self-imposed solitude? Here are suggested activities to enjoy while in cocoon mode:

1. Sign up for Netflix and catch up on movie watching.
2. Pick five new recipes and make a new meal each day of the week. Or, if you don't enjoy cooking, make use of all those takeout menus left on your doorstep by ordering from a different place every night until you find your favorite.
3. Renew your library card and start checking out books on any subject that interests you (from beginner magic tricks to poker to quilting and/or songwriting, you decide!)
4. Purchase a new exercise DVD (tai chi, Pilates, strip aerobics, anyone?) and move that body to a new Movin' On groove.
5. Organize your junk drawer.

Butterfly Mode

You've been that slow-moving caterpillar, you've even embraced cocoon mode, and now you're just bursting to break out of your old life and immerse yourself in your fabulous new one. If this sounds familiar, congratulations! You are in butterfly mode, which also means you've got some serious Movin' On mojo. You've already figured out that in order to live and love your life, it's out with the old and in with the new. Making peace with your past was the first step. Letting go of your identity with your ex was second. Living and loving your life in the *now* is the next order of business. And for you, all signs point to *Go!* It's now time to move on to step four, which is all about reclaiming your space.

RECOMMENDED BUTTERFLY BEHAVIOR

Ready to paint the town red? The following are some suggested activities for your bold butterfly self (and anyone daring enough to join you!):

1. Check out that hot new club everyone's talking about. Scope out the scene, ask some cutie to dance, and kick your Movin' On groove into high gear.
2. Get a makeover at one of those department-store beauty counters. Then put on your most fabulous outfit and strut your stuff around town for the day. Just for fun, keep track of all the heads you turn.
3. If the weather's nice, gathers your g.f.'s and enjoy a picnic in the park, at the beach, or anywhere else you can enjoy the scenery (both nature *and* cute guys!).
4. Embrace your inner child by going out bike riding, roller skating, or swinging on a swing at your local park or playground. Just do something fun that hopefully makes you smile and laugh.

5. Recruit your Woo-Hoo Crew for a night of karaoke at your local dive bar. You don't have to have a good voice to belt out your fave eighties tune, a Sinatra classic, or one of Neil Diamond's greatest hits. Just have fun. (It's contagious!)

Reclaiming Your Space

If you held your Movin' On party at your place, chances are your home is now filled with the fabulously warm, positive energy of your friends and loved ones. (If not, no worries.) It's this energy we're going to channel as you reclaim your space. It's not just the physical space around you that I'm talking about reclaiming. In order to get back to the business of you, you're gonna need to reclaim your emotional space, too. (Don't worry, I'll show you how.)

Clean House

So far, you've been thorough in exorcising your ex from your home life. You've gotten rid of his physical stuff, removed ex-boyfriend residue from your residence (and your heart), and in addition to the bed, you've hopefully taken back your closet, refrigerator, and shower caddy (no more two-in-one shampoo for you!). You may have even smudged, replaced your sorry breakup vibe with a shinier, happier vibe, and moved furniture around to erase any memory of *what went where* while *he* was in your life. By now, your home environment is most likely feeling remarkably drama-free. But we're not done just yet. No, to ensure the ex-boyfriend blues don't return, we've gotta do one last exorcism:

○ Smudge your place one more time. (Better safe than sorry!)

○ Look under your bed, in the back of your closets, in the pantry, and under the bathroom sink to ensure all evidence of your ex is gone (for good!).

○ Go through your closet again and get rid of anything that either reminds you of your ex or no longer suits the Fabulous New You that's about to emerge. Say *So long* to those skinny jeans that mock you instead of inspiring you (that curve-denying bulky sweater you've had since college deserves a similar fate), and be sure to toss that boxy blazer your mom or your ex thought was perfect for job interviews. Buh-bye!

○ Replace any remaining photos of you either with your ex (no matter how good your hair looks in the picture) or in an ex-friendly moment with photos of you in Movin' On mode (and if you have to, gather your Woo-Hoo Crew for an impromptu photo shoot!).

Get in Touch with Your Inner Martha

After you've cleansed your castle one last time, you're ready for the next step in reclaiming your space. It's time to get in touch with your inner Martha (Stewart, that is!). Yes, you my friend are about to embark upon a space-reclaiming extravaganza. (Even if you never lived with your ex, you'll still benefit from making over your space while in Movin' On mode.) Whether you're looking for an arts-and-crafts project to spruce up your space, or you're toying with the new flooring-and-lighting project you've had in mind, or you've been flipping through that Pottery Barn catalog daydreaming of a new sofa, love seat, and coffee table, it's time to channel your domestic diva.

Regardless of what type of project you want to pursue, the following are some suggested activities you can easily take on in your spare time:

Repaint your place Maybe your walls just need a fresh coat of paint or maybe each room in your home is dying to express some individuality. A visit to your local paint store, Home Depot, or Target should inspire your inner artist. From colors to textures to wallpaper, borders, and stencils (not to mention crown moldings!), you can definitely reclaim your space with a can or two of paint and some other basic home improvement tools. (If you've never painted before, get some tips from your paint store and then organize a painting party with your friends.)

Redo one room Is there one particular room in your home that is in dire need of a facelift? Maybe your bathroom needs new fixtures and accessories. Or your bedroom desperately needs new bedding, pillows, and some of that Movin' On mojo. Or your living room has been suffering far too long in silence without a decent entertainment center, burdened instead with that sagging bookcase and that old lumpy couch. If the rest of your place feels fabulous with the exception of that one room, then there's no denying it—a room-specific renovation is in order. Look through home-improvement magazines to see what strikes your fancy. Watch those home-makeover shows to get some cost-saving tips. Shop the furniture sales to get a good deal. And then breathe new life into your bedroom, bathroom, and/or breakfast nook by giving it a much-needed makeover. You'll be surprised how much of a difference redecorating one room will make to your home's overall atmosphere.

Express your individuality This one's especially important if you used to live with your ex because oftentimes cohabitation comes with a cost—your individuality.

If so, now's the time to reclaim your spark by expressing yourself in every room of your home. Even if it's just a new centerpiece, accent pillows, end table, or piece of wall art, you deserve to look around your home and feel it reflects your style, your taste, and your personality. You don't have to spend an arm and a leg to do so. Scour the classifieds, CraigsList.com, yard sales, estate sales, secondhand stores, or your Sunday paper's store sales to get a great deal on whatever you might need to help you express yourself throughout your home. (You *can* redecorate on a budget!)

The Big Finish And maybe, just maybe, you've got something bigger planned. Like tearing out that old carpet and putting in hardwood floors. Or replacing that harsh lighting with something more mellow like ceiling fans, dimmer switches, and new lamps. Or scraping off all that cottage cheese from the ceilings and enjoying a smoother, sleeker look. Of course, these kinds of projects require more money and the hiring of professionals. But if it fits your budget and is something your landlord or homeowners' association allows, go for it!

RECLAIMING YOUR SPACE WITH A ROOMMATE

If you've got a roommate, be sure to consult her before making any major changes to your living space. First, explain why you feel the need to make space-reclaiming changes. (She's been through a breakup or two. She should understand!) Then share your ideas and try to get her input or encourage her involvement. If she remains resistant to change, focus on fixing up your bedroom for now. Other changes may follow as your roommate gets used to the idea of reclaiming your joint space.

Part of living and loving your life right now lies in loving your living space. It's important to take the time and effort to make your home as *you* as possible. Doing what you can to celebrate your life right now will show the universe (and everyone around you) just how well you're doing in Movin' On mode. (And in the process you just might inspire someone else to wake up, break up, and move on from a relationship that no longer works for her.)

Make Your List (and Check It Twice!)

Ready for a fun assignment? This one is equally important when it comes to reclaiming your space, only the space I'm now referring to is *emotional* space. It's time to start thinking about what you may eventually look for in a member of the opposite sex. The question of whether you're ready to date right now is irrelevant. All I want you to do is apply some of those hard-earned breakup lessons you've been learning along the road to recovery to your ideas about a future partner.

Are you game? (The answer's *Yes.*) Okay, get out your journal and make a list of seven to ten traits and qualities that are important to you in a potential life partner. Unlike the list you may or may not have made when you were younger, this list probably (okay, *hopefully*) will not include things like *a rad car, a killer bod, at least 6-feet tall,* and/or *a trust fund.* No, this list is more practical and may include qualities you never before knew were important to you but that are now incredibly valuable as you continue in Movin' On mode. Here is the list I made while recovering from my Big Breakup.

Lisa's List
Traits I Hope to Find in My Perfect Partner

1. Kind-hearted (someone who genuinely cares about people and the world around him)

2. Humble (someone who doesn't spend all his time being self-involved)
3. Self-aware (he should be comfortable with himself and know who he is)
4. Emotionally available (and able to share himself with me)
5. Goal-oriented (*not* the same as ridiculously ambitious)
6. Communicative (please!)
7. An equal (pretty please!)
8. Sense of humor (I know everyone says it, but I really mean it!)
9. A genuine zest for life (and the desire to share it)
10. Someone who's capable of loving me on the same level that I love him (no more excess baggage!)

Even if the idea of dating is the furthest thing from your mind, this exercise is still helpful to your recovery because it helps shape the kind of partner you'll eventually attract. It also helps apply what you've learned from your last relationship to what you're looking for in the next one. So make your list.

RECOVERY ℞

Looking for a pick-me-up that'll help pick others up, too? Get domestic! Mix up a batch of brownies, cookies, or cupcakes and then deliver them to your neighbors, family members, friends, and/or coworkers. It'll brighten their day *and* give you a lift as well.

After my Big Breakup, I realized I no longer wanted to date someone who was unwilling to deal with his emotional baggage. It was perfectly okay to have emotional baggage, but I wanted to find someone like me who was willing to acknowledge the pain of the past as just that—part of the past—and be healthy enough to have moved on from it. As I started dating again, I began adding other qualities to my list as they revealed their importance to me. For example, I discovered that while self-confidence was important to me, self-awareness was more desirable. Dating someone who was kind to me was nice, but even better was dating someone who was also kind to the world around us. I think you'll find that you, too, start making these kinds of distinctions as you continue in Movin' On mode.

The Business of You

Since the title of this chapter is "Getting Back to the Business of You," let's do just that—focus on you for a minute. Is there anything you felt you had to give up in your last relationship that you would like to reclaim? Or is there something you wanted to pursue or try that for one reason or another you just didn't because of your last relationship? For example, maybe you wanted to get certified to scuba dive, but your ex didn't like the water. Or maybe you used to rollerblade all the time, but your ex liked to hike instead so your blades are somewhere in the back of your closet just waiting to be dusted off and taken out for a spin. (If so, dust them off and go for it!) Or maybe once upon a time (long before Mr. Ex), you loved to make jewelry but stopped because it was so time-consuming and took up too much space and being in a relationship was all you had the energy for (not to mention the fact that you had to clear space for all of Mr. Ex's junk). Why not pick up those old hobbies or private passions? Now is the perfect time to take on a new challenge, rediscover an old love, or *finally* do that thing you've always talked about. Chances are that you have something in mind (or maybe it will come to you in the coming days or weeks).

For the record, reclaiming your space isn't just about making over where you live and reconnecting to old hobbies and interests. It can also apply to new directions you never thought of before (or that have just been buried for far too long). As you move through Movin' On mode, pay attention to any new thoughts and/or ideas that spring up. Be mindful of any new passions or interests that emerge. And remind yourself that you're now free to pursue them—or to at least start *considering* them. The following are some possible life changes you may want to think about as you continue to reclaim your space:

Go back to school Whether you want to take one class or earn a whole new degree is up to you!

Make a career switch You can change companies, industries, or professions, depending on your comfort level and desire.

Change your body, change your life Can't make peace with what the mirror and scale say? Now may be the perfect time to enlist the help of experts, including a personal trainer, a nutritionist, and/or a support group (either online or in person) to help you change your body and life for good. Weight Watchers, your neighborhood gym, and/or eDiets.com are all great places to get started.

Relocate If you're a butterfly in need of new horizons, the best change for you just might be a change in scenery. That might mean moving to a new home, getting or ditching a roommate, or maybe, just maybe, relocating to a new city. Only you will know for sure what type of relocation will help you reclaim your space. It's time to start being open to the amazing possibilities!

Just because you've started thinking about making some changes doesn't mean they have to happen overnight. Give yourself time to mull things over, consider all the possibilities, do your research, and really make an educated decision before diving into a life-altering change. For now, it may be enough just to be thinking about changing things up. I'll talk more about shaking up your life in Chapter 8. (For now, mull away!)

Revisiting Your Fabulous Factor

It's probably been a while since you last looked at your Fabulous Factor list. But I want you to open your journal and find it. First, I want you to review what's already there. Give yourself time to process each thing on the list. By the time you get to the last item, you should be feeling pretty fabulous about yourself (Yes? No? Maybe?). Next, I want you to add at least three new things to your list. Start with something fabulous that you're just discovering about yourself, like *I finally lost those ten pounds I gained during my breakup recovery and look better than ever,* or *I'm living and loving every moment of cocoon mode,* or *I'm a beautiful butterfly ready to spread my wings and fly!*

Really take some time with your list. You've earned your bragging rights, so go for it. When you're done, take a moment to celebrate exactly where you are right now in life. Whether you're that slow-moving caterpillar, are comfortably nestled in your recovery cocoon, or are taking your first few breaths of new life into your butterfly lungs, cherish these moments. Celebrate them! You can even pat yourself on the back for everything you've been through. And then turn the page. The best is (still) yet to come.

between-chapter *check-in*

This chapter has covered a variety of topics—from assessing where you are in Movin' On mode to reclaiming your space to rediscovering your Fabulous Factor. Below (or in your journal) I want you to write down what you found easiest to tackle, and then what was most challenging for you.

Example: *I loved reclaiming my space. I invited all my g.f.'s over and we had a painting party and ordered pizza. Now my place looks amazing! The thing I'm struggling with most is that I have no interest in meeting someone new right now. I'm happy in my little cocoon. I think moving on from that will be hard for me.*

DATE  _____

_____

_____

_____

_____

_____

CHAPTER EIGHT

LIVE/LOVE YOUR LIFE
aka give SINGLE GALS
a good name

Once upon a time, you may have thought that being single was a life sentence. Right after your breakup, you may have even viewed it as synonymous with being alone, lonely, or otherwise pathetic. But by now, you hopefully know better. In fact, you're most likely getting to a place in Movin' On mode where you can fully embrace being single for all the amazing attributes that come with it.

If you're not there quite yet, don't worry. That's what this chapter is all about—learning to look at your single status in a new light and discovering all the ways to rejoice in it. After all, there's a good chance it's temporary. If what you truly desire is to settle down, get married (or at least find a life partner), and/or have children, you most likely will achieve that. In the meantime, why wait for *some guy* to complete your life picture? Why not celebrate this time for what it is—a little decadent and a whole lot of fun?

In case you've been living under a single-gal rock (or are still in caterpillar mode), let me remind you of something. The joys of being single are endless. Staying out 'til 3 A.M. with your girlfriends. Running off for the weekend without a second thought. Switching careers without worrying about how it will affect anyone but you. Dating wildly different types of men until you find the one that best fits you. Curling up on a Saturday night (or a lazy Sunday afternoon) with a good book, your fave movie, or a glass of wine while you enjoy some much-needed solitude after a busy week at work. Meeting cute strangers in the supermarket express line, at the twenty-four-hour diner you and your girlfriends frequent at 2 A.M., in the seat next to you on the subway. Living life according to your own rules (or tossing the rule book out the window and winging it!).

Welcome to the Single State, Population You

Happy *single and ready to mingle* gals everywhere know that being single is a state of mind. And it can be an incredibly rewarding state if you celebrate it right here and now, as your life is in this very moment. You don't need to lose twenty pounds, be debt free, have tons of boyfriends, or land your dream job to enjoy being single. You just need to make peace with any lingering single stigma you may hold onto, embrace your sense of adventure, and be open to the amazing possibilities. It's time to celebrate the fact that you have yet to meet Mr. Right (and that you're far too fabulous to settle for Mr. So-So), that you are not yet saddled with the responsibilities that come with marriage or motherhood—don't worry, there's still time if you're interested—

and to realize that regardless of your age, life has not passed you by. In fact, your life is right here waiting for you. It's up to you to embrace it, celebrate it, and say *Thank God!* It's time to give thanks for being exactly where you are right now (and while you're at it, give thanks for the one who got away, too!).

Giving single gals a good name is easy, especially when you know where to find like-minded individuals—both online and off. The following are some useful online resources for living (and loving) the single life.

Online Resources for the Savvy Single

www.quirkyalone.net

You don't have to be a social misfit to be a quirkyalone. In fact, according to the Web site, the term "quirkyalone" simply refers to "A person who enjoys being single (but is not opposed to being in a relationship) and generally prefers to be alone rather than dating for the sake of being in a couple." If that sounds familiar, check out this Web site, where you can chat with other like-minded individuals in the online community, buy the book *QuirkyAlone: A Manifesto for Uncompromising Romantics*, and even take part in International QuirkyAlone Day on, you guessed it, February 14!

www.cuddleparty.com

While being single rocks, sometimes you can feel a little touch deprived. Fear not, my fabulous single friends! A cuddle party just might be what the doctor ordered. Founders Reid and Marcia facilitate cuddle parties all over the United States and even parts of Canada. So just what is a cuddle party? It's a safe and nurturing environment where healthy and happy people gather to cuddle for an evening (fully clothed, of course!). Hey, don't knock it 'til you try it.

www.simplyseductress.com

If the idea of cuddling for a night with complete strangers creeps you out, why not gather the girls and get in touch with your inner seductress? Founder Tara Moore combines her love of dancing with her passion for helping women connect to their own innate sensuality by offering workshops, online resources, and tools dedicated to self-improvement and empowerment.

www.selfnurture.com

If you're looking for an online destination that celebrates the upside of being single, look no further! Singles enthusiast Jean Zartner launched her Web site in hopes of helping others celebrate their single selves. SelfNurture.com features articles, tips, and other resources for celebrating life in the single state.

It's also important to realize that in embracing your single self, you are not rebuffing your desire for a relationship or your hopes of one day having children. You can still want those things. But it's time to let go of the idea that until you have them, you are not healthy, happy, and/or whole. Or that your married-with-children friends are somehow better than you for being where they are compared to where you are in life.

But, you may be saying, *being married looks so amazing.* Or, you might be thinking, *Being a mother must be fantastic. I'm really missing out!*

RECOVERY R̪

Miss spending time with your best married-with-child friend? Chances are she misses you, too. Call her up or shoot her an e-mail to arrange a play date for the two of you (without babies, husbands, or anyone else). Sneak off for afternoon tea or happy hour or a hike or a mani-pedi. Just pick somewhere that the two of you can have quality time without distraction to catch up on each other's busy lives. You'll both return to your respective lives feeling re-energized and ready to conquer the world!

Stop right there. While it's perfectly normal to *occasionally* envy those coupled up or married-with-child friends, guess what? They envy you, too! You have freedom they only vaguely remember. To them, your life just may look like a never-ending joy ride that they sometimes fantasize about trading their firstborn for. Unlike them, you get to sneak off to a movie by yourself on a moment's notice (without having to line up a babysitter). Go dancing with your single gal pals 'til the wee hours of the morning (without having to ask your man if he'll stay home and watch the kids). Take off on that singles ski weekend (without having to clear it with the family finance department *plus* you get the option of flirting with the sexy ski instructor, the cutie on the chair lift, *and* that snowboarding hottie on the slopes).

WHAT'S ON A SINGLE GAL'S BOOKSHELF?

Why You're Still Single: Things Your Friends Would Tell You If You Promised Not to Get Mad, by Evan Marc Katz and Linda Holmes

Don't let the title fool you. This isn't a book blaming you for being single. Rather, it's a refreshingly funny he said/she said take on the joys, perils, and truths of being single from two sharp-witted writers who also happen to be single.

My Own Private Idaho (Okay, Montana)

Once upon a time, I was a 30-year-old single gal who thought life just might have passed me by. Both of my best friends were married and starting families. And yet there I was, staring down the barrel of my Big Breakup. Not only was I not married or having children, I couldn't even achieve a successful relationship. I was convinced that I was somehow a failure at love (and possibly at life) and that I might as well just curl up and die a sad spinster. (Sound a bit dramatic? This was probably during one of those panic attacks every single thirty-something woman feels at one time or another. Bear with me. It gets better!)

And then one day I had this epiphany. I was sitting on my girlfriend's couch feeling particularly frustrated in my search for Mr. Right. My fellow single gal was doing her best to cheer me up. (Thanks, Mel!) I think she said something along the lines of, *Don't worry, Lisa. He's out there.*

What is it about that line? Depending upon how we're feeling, it either serves as an emotional life preserver that just might revive our dreams or feels like a dull dagger slowly slicing and dicing its way through what's left of our dwindling hope. On that day, it felt like the dagger. And that's when I had the epiphany. Most likely it had been brewing for years, cultivated by being the only single person at one-too-many dinner parties or family gatherings where a married-with-child friend, acquaintance, or long-lost relative would inevitably shoot me that familiar puzzled look, punctuated by the question *Why are you still single?* And always, after I managed to shrug and say, *I just haven't met the right guy yet*, their expression would morph into a reassuring smile, followed by those words: *Don't worry, he's out there.*

I don't want to lie anymore, I remember saying to my girlfriend who just looked at me, uncertain of what I was getting at. *Maybe he's out there, maybe he's not. But I just don't want to lie to myself anymore.*

It was that simple for me. I didn't want to spend any more time walking through life feeling like I was in any way less than the person next to me just because she happened to wear a ring on her left hand. I no longer had the energy to bang my head against the wall in frustration over the fact that I had yet to meet my perfect partner. For sanity's sake, I had to stop looking in the mirror and pitying the beautiful life I had just because it didn't involve a husband or a baby.

With that little epiphany, I retired my search for Mr. Right and set my sights on a more attainable goal—creating a life that I could live and love with or without a man. For me, that meant quitting my job, renting out my expensive Southern California condo, putting my belongings in storage, and retreating to my childhood roots in the Montana wilderness for the summer, something I'd always talked about doing but until then, hadn't had the guts to go for. (Talk about shaking things up!) There, I reconnected with my extended family, found a sense of peace under the wide-open skies with the tall mountain peaks in every direction, and made friends with an incredible crew of people who were also living and loving life on their own terms. I hiked. I practiced yoga and Pilates. I patiently sat in traffic jams behind herds of bison (sure beats rush-hour traffic on the 405 freeway any day!).

In opening myself up to these new experiences, the universe opened itself up to me. I started getting more and more freelance writing gigs that I could do from anywhere. Men started to take notice of me more frequently (and the caliber of interested parties improved). With each passing day, I fell deeper and deeper in love with the way I was choosing to lead my new life. I eventually returned to California, where

I moved in with friends in my fave artsy neighborhood and created my own little family. We cooked together, stayed up late talking, laughing, and watching bad television, and coaxed each other's creative projects into existence—including this book. (Thanks, Chris and Renee!) I felt like I finally found the support system I had always wanted and needed (but had only been looking for in a man). I realized that *this* was a life I could get on board with—a life that celebrated me and my incredible independence. One that in no way relied on a romantic relationship to complete me but still remained open to the possibility of love. (I just wasn't holding my breath and turning blue anymore.)

Somewhere along this journey, my conversations with those married-with-children friends changed, too. Whereas they once revolved around the joys of motherhood and marital bliss, they now were more honest. More genuine. During one of our typical confessional phone calls, my best married-with-child friend actually confided in me, "Lisa, I'm missing my entire thirties!" Here I'd spent years envying her, thinking she had it all and that I was missing out. But you know what? I was now in a position to see that we both had enviable lives. Just as she was lucky to find her husband in her twenties, have a baby by 30, and spend her thirties raising that child (in the meantime making motherhood look absolutely amazing), I, too, was lucky. In not meeting Mr. Right in my twenties, I got to date around, go to Europe by myself, enjoy an endless stream of fun and fabulous Friday and Saturday nights without a curfew or guilt, buy my first home on my own (self sufficiency *rocks*!), date/kiss/sleep with a variety of exciting, interesting, amazing men (sorry, Mom and Dad!), quit my well-paying stable day job to pursue freelance work without having to clear it with anyone but myself, travel to Montana for the summer without permission or consequence (and decide to return the following summer without having to clear it with my partner), and sleep as late as I wanted to on the weekends without anyone waking me up wanting to watch cartoons, need help fixing breakfast, or change yet another dirty diaper. Sure, there would be plenty of time for that in the future, if that was what I wanted. But in the meantime, I began to see just how lucky I was.

And how lucky are you? (The answer is *very*!)

The Single Gal Roller Coaster

Of course, loving your single gal life doesn't mean there won't be moments of doubt or despair. Just because you embrace your life doesn't mean it's always going to be rosy. After a string of bad dates, when you have a really trying week at work, when the umpteenth Saturday night rolls around and you don't have any plans, of course you're going to doubt the celebratory nature of being single. But that's just the way it goes. Your coupled-up friends go through relationship ruts. Your married-with-children friends get overwhelmed with parenthood or pissed off at their partners and secretly wish they were single for just a day or two (or a month). The grass may not always be greener, but it sure can look like it sometimes. (Don't worry, it's all perfectly normal.)

Still think your coupled-up friends have it made in the shade? The following are some common myths about the plusses of partnership and the reality checks you should consider.

Myth-Busting *Happily Ever After*

Myth *Dual incomes rock.*

Reality Sure, having two incomes seems better than one. But oftentimes being part of a partnership involves double the debt (for instance, twice the student loan payments, car loans, and a bigger mortgage for a larger family).

Translation Your single gal income is just right for right now!

Myth *Having children around the same time your friends do is super cool and fun.*

Reality Having children just because your friends are having them is not enough reason to procreate before you're ready. And beating yourself up when you receive your umpteenth baby shower invite while you're still *single and ready to mingle* is another no-no you should avoid.

Translation Be happy for where your friends are in their lives, but also see your amazing life for all its awesome attributes.

Myth *Being married far outweighs being single.*

Reality Being married can be amazing. But being single can be equally amazing. And let's face it—marrying the wrong person just to say you're married or so that you, too, can have a ring on your hand is worse than any string of bad dates or dating dry spell. (And spending time on your own, getting to know yourself, will make you a better partner once you do meet Mr. Right!)

Translation Celebrate the state you currently reside in.

> *movin' on secret #3*
> Like attracts like. Wouldn't you rather attract someone fantastic than someone who's just as bored and bitter as you may be? (The answer's *yes*.)

The key to having a wonderful life is in living and loving your life as it is right now. Not only will you be happier in the long run, but you're more likely to attract a happy, healthy, whole individual when you're living and loving your life than when you're miserable, mopey, and mad about being single.

The Bar Stool Rule

Picture this. You're sitting at a bar looking super sexy. There are two guys across from you. One is handsome, happy, and full of energy. The other is slouched, sad, and bordering on pathetic. Which guy do you want to talk to? (If you answered this one correctly, you'll send a drink on over to the happy hottie, and before you know it, he'll be fixing his emotionally available gaze on you. If you're drawn to the slouching sad sap, well, we've still got a lot of work to do.)

Now, apply that Bar Stool Rule to your own life. Give yourself permission to sit up straight, smile, and project the most amazing and authentic *You* possible. And not just at the bar. But when you're walking down the street. Or at work. Or at the gym. Or on the freeway or subway. Even at home. The more you put your best *You* out there, the more comfortable it will become (and the more likely other people are to take notice of and be inspired by the new and improved You).

Shaking Things Up

If you just can't get on board with your life as it is, chances are that no man's going to be able to fix that. Instead, you've got to figure out how to remedy the situation yourself.

What can you do right now to make your life better/more satisfying/happier?

It just might be time to shake things up.

Exactly how do you shake things up? That depends on what part of you or your life needs shaking up. Read on to identify which area of your life might be in need of a Movin' On makeover.

You Hate Your Job

In a rut at work? Stop complaining and *do* something about it! Yes, change can be scary. But you know what? You survived your Big Breakup. Looking for a new and better job and adjusting to the changes that accompany it is nothing compared to what you've been through. Or, if changing jobs isn't an option at the moment, then change the way you feel about going to work. Accept that it's just a paycheck (for now anyway) and that it's up to you to find fulfillment elsewhere. Or ask your boss for more responsibility, a new challenge, or permission to take a career-oriented class or seminar if that'll make your 9 to 5 life more meaningful. (Remember, you gotta love your life right now!)

You Hate Where You Live

Sick of your living space? If you can afford it and it makes good sense, move. Or if you're tired of renting, look into buying your first (or second) home. It may sound daunting, but it just may be doable (and for less than you think!). If moving isn't an option, recruit your Woo-Hoo Crew and shake up your place. Move around furniture (or buy a new piece or two), paint the walls new and fresh colors (if you haven't already), apply the rules of feng shui and see if that does the trick. Being happy at home is crucial to living and loving your life. So do whatever it takes to make the place you come home to every night work for you. You might just need to buy yourself flowers once a week for the dining room table or treat yourself to a new set of dishes you can look forward to eating off of, or brighten up your space with new curtains.

You Hate Your Love Life (or Lack Thereof)

In a dating desert? Invite your Woo-Hoo Crew over for a night of cocktails and online dating. Have your g.f.'s do your hair and makeup (and if they want to shake things up, they can do the same), put on a fab outfit, and take some saucy digital pictures. Upload them to the dating site(s) of choice, then drink cocktails while coming up with the most amazing online profile. Mix up another batch of cocktails and surf the site for potential love connections or just have fun perusing the possibilities. Or, if online dating makes you want to dry heave (believe me, I've been there), sign up for a local singles event like speed dating or a cuddle party. Or if you're the outdoorsy type, do some research and find out if the local Sierra Club has activities for singles. And here's a novel idea. Why not gather your Woo-Hoo Crew and hit the bar scene, arts festival, or some other target-rich environment where you're likely to meet plenty of *single and ready to mingle* men? (Can't hurt!)

Movin' On Vocabulary

Target-Rich Environment Any location where *single and ready to mingle* ladies will find a decent selection of quality *single and ready to mingle* men. For example, a dive bar may be target-rich, but is that the target you're aiming for? If not, set your sights a little higher. Think charity fundraiser. Evening activities at your local museum. Volunteering for your local public radio station pledge drive. Or just volunteering. (Get creative!)

The Scarcity Excuse The belief that there are no good single men "out there" and that explains why you're still single. (It's a myth. Don't buy the hype!)

The Numbers Game A healthy approach to dating that reminds *single and ready to mingle* gals that in order to meet someone fabulous, they may just have to meet a few not-so-fabulous guys along the way (but it's sooo worth the time and effort!).

Wing Girl Someone who aids in the savvy single gal's search for eligible dating candidates by making introductions, starting conversations, and then fading into the background.

You're Bored with Your Daily Routine

Does your life seem like a never-ending cycle of *work, home, eat, sleep, repeat*? Your routine just may be in a rut. Pick up a catalog from your local community college or Learning Annex, and enroll in the class that most strikes your fancy. Whether it's learning a new language, taking a dance class (swing, salsa, tango, anyone?!), or enrolling in a spicy cooking class, you never know who you might meet or what you might learn. And you don't have to make a love connection for it to be worthwhile. Making new friends, acquiring a new skill, or just exploring a new hobby can make a world of difference if you're looking to shake up your life.

Another Way to Shake Things Up

To really live and love your life, you need to ask yourself what you're waiting on a man to provide. And no, I'm not talking about a wedding ring or a baby. I'm talking about more basic things that you've always just assumed a man would bring into your relationship and therefore you have yet to provide them for yourself. Like a nice set of steak knives. Or camping gear. Or DSL. Or new furniture. For me, I had always relied upon a boyfriend to provide the entertainment system. Whenever I was dating someone, I enjoyed surround sound, crystal clear picture on a big screen, and cable television. In between boyfriends, I found myself squinting at my tiny television without cable and carting a clunky CD player from room to room to listen to music. I kept putting off buying these things for myself, convinced that any minute now *some guy* was going to come along and provide them for me.

And then one day I just decided to go out and get what I wanted for myself. I scoured the newspaper ads to find a multi-disc player and surround sound system in my price range. I paid for it with my hard-earned money. And soon enough, I was watching movies with my very own surround sound. Shuffling music on my very own five-disc CD player. I even got cable television for my single self. It was a small step for womankind, but a major step for me.

Can you think of anything you might be waiting on a man to provide for you? Is it something you'd be willing to invest a little money (and/or time) in to provide for yourself? It's such a small gesture with an incredibly big reward. By giving yourself this gift, you're proving to the universe (and yourself) that you believe you deserve to live and love your life on your own terms.

And it's not just about household items. What else are you postponing until The One comes into your life? Taking a well-deserved vacation? Going back to school? Making a career change? Sometimes we get so hung up on the life we think we'll start leading once Mr. Right comes along that we forget the importance of making our lives the best they can possibly be in the meantime. Why should you have to wait for *some guy* to buy that couch, take that vacation, or make that career change? You don't have to! Do it now while you don't have to ask permission/clear it with your partner/fit it into the family budget. It's your life—you should love it as much as humanly possible.

Ready to take that much-needed vacation but don't feel comfortable going alone? The following are some suggested ways to travel.

Travel Tips for the Savvy Single Gal

○ Recruit a friend or family member to go with you. Even if you don't spend every waking moment together, you'll still feel more comfortable knowing you're not totally alone in a strange locale.

○ Sign up for a singles-oriented vacation, cruise, or tour. You don't have to make a love connection to enjoy the company of like-minded singles!

○ Visit family and/or friends you haven't seen in a long time. You don't have to travel abroad or go someplace exotic to feel like you're on vacation!

○ Find a host family. If you want to go someplace you've never been and can't recruit anyone to join you, do some online research and find a host family you might be able to stay with. *www.servas.org* is an international organization that connects travelers from all over the world with host families in different countries.

The Curse of The One

Have you been searching for The One your entire life? Or maybe your quest is more recent but nonetheless urgent. Worse still, does it seem like everyone around you has easily found their perfect partner and, just like that horrible game of musical chairs when you were a kid, you're the only one left standing without a chair (or a partner) when the music stops?

movin' on secret #4

If you're obsessively looking for The One, you won't find him.

If you think the universe is mocking you by sending you on yet another bad date with some dork or jerk or clueless cad, you just might be on to something. While the universe is notorious for rewarding our hard work, it's also known for having a wicked sense of humor, especially when it comes to our pursuit of love. Look too hard and you won't find it. Invest too much of your energy, and all you'll have to show for your efforts is a string of disappointing dates and a major dose of frustration.

But don't give up hope. That's the worst thing you could do. You just have to temper your expectations. Take some of that focus off your search, and invest it back into living and loving your life. The universe likes that (and so do guys!). By showing the universe (and men) that you're open to love but not chasing it like a heat-seeking missile, you're embracing your life in the now while remaining open to the possibilities.

After retiring my obsessive search for The One and falling in love with life on my own, I found that I was attracting men like crazy. Immediately, I weighed myself. No, I hadn't lost those nagging twenty pounds. I checked my bank statement. Nope, hadn't won the lottery either (or even finished paying off my credit card). And yet the men kept appearing, smiling, asking for my name or number, leaning in to kiss me. *What was going on?* I wondered. *Oh yeah*, I realized. *I'm not looking.*

And then something even more bizarre happened. Somewhere between the great kisser at my favorite bar and the sexy rough-around-the-edges writer I had exchanged numbers with at my neighborhood coffeehouse, I met Mr. XY. He just happened to be sitting with friends at the table next to my girlfriend and me at our neighborhood bar/lounge. She and I had come to listen to the music and hoped that my fabulously talented friend (you rock, Renee!) would get invited to sing with the lounge's resident duo. He and his friends had come to have a few drinks and catch up on old times. My girlfriend sang. Mr. XY and I talked. It was easy. Comfortable. Fun. And I was more than willing to leave it at that.

But when Mr. XY got up to leave later that evening, he asked for my number. He would later tell me that he too had pondered just walking away, having enjoyed our conversation but not needing to take it to the next level. Like me, he was in a space where he was living and loving his life on his own terms. He wasn't looking either. Even after I gave Mr. XY my card, I dismissed the experience. I never once gave any thought to if or when he might call. So when he called the very next day, I was both surprised and pleased. No games. I liked that.

Now, I tell you about how I met Mr. XY not to brag or make an impossible guarantee that you too will meet Mr. Right once you ease up your search for him. But I tell you about him to remind you of the possibilities and to illustrate the value of lightening up when it comes to men. They'll appreciate it, and you'll discover that it makes your life so much easier (and more enjoyable, too).

So if you need to, put yourself on a dating hiatus. Take time to regroup your emotions. And in the process, cut men some slack. You may find that as a result you'll enjoy your interactions with the opposite sex that much more. You won't always be thinking, *Maybe he's The One.* He may be The One, or he may just be the one on the barstool nearest you, the one ahead of you picking up his dry cleaning, the one closest to you at that rockin' concert, or the one who's smiling at you from the car next to you while stuck in bumper-to-bumper traffic on the freeway. Those "Ones" are equally important because they're terrific practice. They allow us to get our flirt on, figure out the do's and don'ts of our own personal dating strategy, and most importantly, they remind us that there are plenty of possibilities out there. We don't have to settle down (and more importantly settle), get married, and have children with the first guy who makes eye contact with us. We can afford to be picky. To date until we find someone who's a good match for us. To *really* play the numbers game.

At the end of the day, that's what dating's all about. Numbers. Maybe you'll meet someone amazing right away. Or maybe you'll be like most of us and have to meet a handful of (or a hundred) Mr. Wrongs before Mr. Right comes along. Either way, it's fun to be a contestant in the numbers game, isn't it? Sure beats settling for less than you deserve, agreeing to an arranged marriage, or resigning yourself to an early spinsterhood by giving up before you even really get started.

The Scarcity Excuse,
aka How to Change Your Man Karma
in Just Seven Days

Convinced there are no single men left on the planet (or at least any decent ones)? Chances are that you have scarcity issues. And to prove yourself wrong, you need to practice the following exercise for seven days. Every day for the next week, your mission is to initiate a conversation with a new man. If the thought of approaching that cutie you always see at your chiropractor's office feels daunting, start with a less intimidating subject. Ask a guy at the gym what time it is. Then smile, make eye contact, and say thanks. Tell the nice-looking man waiting with you at the crosswalk or the car wash that you like his shoes. Or his watch. Or his tie. (Just pick whatever catches your eye.) Work your way up to the cutie in your chiropractor's office. If you haven't summoned up the strength within the week, don't worry. We'll be repeating this exercise in Chapter 9. In the meantime, just practice talking to men. Soon enough, you'll realize they're *everywhere*!

Finding your perfect partner isn't easy. If it was, everyone would be happily hooked up and there would be no breakups, online dating, or matchmaking services. (And I wouldn't be writing this book.) Just remember, like attracts like. If you're uptight or frustrated by your love life, you'll most likely attract people who either are drawn to drama or enjoy being a doormat. (Alternately, the only thing you'll attract is pet hair and dryer lint as you while away your single gal days on your couch.) That's not what you want or deserve. But if you lighten up and practice patience, you'll most likely attract people (and possibly a partner) who are happy, healthy, and whole. And that's more like it!

Burying the Single Gal Hatchet

Right about now would be a good time to go on record and say that there is nothing wrong with staying single forever, if that's what makes you happy. I know a handful of people who are perfectly content living their lives as perpetual bachelors and bachelorettes. Marriage and babies were never part of their plan. Their lives are just as full and worthwhile and amazing as the lives of their friends who chose to marry, settle down, and have children. If, after surviving your Big Breakup and completing Movin' On mode, you decide that staying single is what's right for you, then congratulations! You are choosing the life that most authentically suits you. And that's all anyone can ever ask of you—to be honest with yourself and your wants, needs, and desires.

Choosing to stay single doesn't mean you'll be alone forever. It just means that you'll most likely create an existence that revolves around relationships other than the romantic. Maybe you'll surround yourself with friends and family. Or you'll find a job that offers a built-in extended family, like teaching or theater, or one that affords a lifetime of adventure and the opportunity to meet new people, like traveling the world as a tour guide or working on a cruise ship.

And don't forget that you can always change your mind. Today you may choose to celebrate your independence. Then, one day in the near or distant future, someone may just come along who makes you rethink those plans. In the meantime, you choose to make the most of your life and that's what's really important. In embracing where you are in life today, you are not waiting for *some guy* to complete you. You're figuring out how to make your life as happy and whole as possible right now. Not only that, you are acknowledging that you will never waste away just because

The One hasn't shown up yet. In the event that Mr. Right doesn't show up (or is just slightly delayed in his arrival), you are making your life happen right now. And in doing so you, my fabulous friend, are doing everything right. Keep up the amazing work (and just keep going). You are such a Movin' On rock star!

between-chapter *check-in*

When you read Chapter 8, what thoughts, feelings, and/or resistance came up for you? Take a moment to write a sentence or two below or in your journal about this chapter. Chances are that you had a strong reaction to at least one (if not more) of the topics tackled. Whether you struggle to let go of your single stigma, are scared to deal with your scarcity issues, or think putting your search for The One on hold is just plain stupid, dive right in and dissect why you think you're having those strong emotions. If you're fully in love with and embracing your single state, write about that, too!

Example: *I just don't think I could ever retire my desire for marriage and kids. But I guess I could lighten up about my approach to finding my perfect partner. And I definitely need to work on my scarcity issues. Looks like I still have a lot of work to do. (And that's just fine!)*

DATE

CHAPTER NINE

the fabulous female's
guide to DATING

there will come a time in your Movin' On recovery when you'll want to date again. Whether that day is today or whether it comes next week, next month, or even next year is up to you. As the keeper of your healed heart, only you will know when the time is right to get back out there. And when you do, you'll want to be prepared for your dating future.

Exactly how do you prepare for your dating future? You make peace with your relationship past. You pay attention to the lessons you've learned (and continue to learn) along the way in your Movin' On recovery. You make sure your heart is sufficiently healed. You also make sure that you're aware of both the kind of guy you're looking to attract and the kind of guy (or guys) you should be avoiding (like the ones you fall for too quickly and then inevitably get burned by).

If the prospect of meeting someone new or filtering out inappropriate candidates in favor of healthy, happy, whole individuals overwhelms you, don't worry. That's what this chapter is all about. Together, we are going to embark on a crash course in dating smarter. That means figuring out how to seek out only the eligible candidates (and quickly and easily filtering through the slackers, bad boys, and emotionally stunted head cases) and ultimately learning how to break up with any lingering bad love habits you may have. If it sounds daunting, don't worry. It's not. In fact, it's going to be pretty easy. Not only that, this chapter will be the absolute best education your healed heart could ever ask for. It's going to help equip you for a relationship future that is as drama-free and joy-filled as possible. That's what you deserve, and that's what we're going to strive for. Now, let's get to work!

A New You, a New Approach to Dating

If your Big Breakup and subsequent Movin' On metamorphosis have taught us anything, it's that you now have a better idea of what you want out of life and what you're not going to settle for anymore (like an unsatisfying relationship with someone who's not your equal). As you open yourself up to dating again and the fabulously endless possibilities, remember that from now on, you're going to date smarter—not harder. The following sections outline a step-by-step guide to dating smarter. By following these simple steps, you will likely enjoy a more fulfilling dating present, not to mention be well on your way to a *happily ever after* future.

Step 1: Be Clear about What You Want

Being clear about where you are in life and what you're looking for in the relationship department is essential to dating smarter. If you clearly state your intentions, it will be that much easier to identify suitable matches, cut down on wasted time (both yours and all those Mr. Wrongs out there), and ultimately achieve your goals. Take a look at the dating scenarios that follow and identify which one best describes your current relationship goals. Then read on to see how you can strive for dating and relationship success given your particular goal.

Scenario #1: You're just not looking for love right now.

If you're still comfy in cocoon mode, don't rush yourself into dating. There's no point in putting yourself out there when you're not ready, willing, and/or able to be your most fabulously authentic and available *You* possible. However, that doesn't mean you have to check into a convent or declare a national state of celibacy. You *can* still take part in the occasional flirt fest, and you're totally allowed to work on your grocery-store game, your latte-line lash batting, and your *shake it don't break it* head-turning strut. After all, practice makes perfect.

Scenario #2: You're not looking for a relationship but are most definitely single and ready to mingle!

Happy and healthy single ladies everywhere know that the key to eventually finding a perfect partner lies in playing the numbers game. How else will you know what you really want in a mate if you haven't done your research? And the best research for a *single and ready to mingle* gal like you is to date, date, date (and/or flirt, flirt, flirt!). Your efforts should be focused on making eye contact and initiating conversation with the opposite sex wherever you go, from the bank to the bar to the gym to the grocery store.

Contrary to the widely believed (and completely false) scarcity excuse, men *are* everywhere. It's up to you to meet them, filter out the unavailable and undesirable ones, and flirt with the amazing and available ones who just might want to ask you out. If what you genuinely desire is a fulfilling and active social life, then you'll want to further increase your odds of meeting date-worthy candidates by expanding your search to online dating as well as the in-person approach. Just be sure to avoid marriage-minded dating sites like *www.eharmony.com* and *www.perfectmatch.com*. Instead, focus on more casual dating sites like *www.itsjustcoffee.com* (a site that believes the first date should be as simple as a cup of coffee and a casual chat) and the brilliant multitasking site *www.flirtingintraffic.com* (a perfect hybrid of online dating and freeway flirting!). When it comes to online dating, make sure that your online profile accurately reflects your dating intentions, whatever they may be (and continue to update and refine your profile as your wants and needs change).

Scenario #3: You're ready to settle down, possibly get married, and eventually have children.

If you're on a monogamy and/or marriage-minded mission, you will most definitely want to steer clear of casual daters, players, and boys who like booty calls. You may also want to enlist the help of a matchmaker, sign up for those marriage-minded sites mentioned in the previous section, and regularly attend singles events. Above all else, you should *always* be prepared to put your best *You* out there.

DATING TIP: THE 50/50 FACTOR

Don't be in too much of a rush to get married. After all, 50 percent of marriages fail. In order to be one of the success stories, you need to know who you are. You have to love your life with or without a man, date smart, and *only* agree to a lifelong commitment with someone whom you not only love but whom you actually like and can visualize having a successful and happy life with. (You're far too fabulous to settle for anything less!)

Whether you know it or not, there *are* still *single and ready to mingle* men out there who want to settle down and get married and who would love to find a fabulous partner like you. In order to meet them, though, you need to be willing to do the work, put in the time, and not get frustrated or sidetracked when things don't go your way. (Check out the section entitled "Secret Strategies of the Numbers Game" on page 197.) And repeat this mantra: Ya gotta be in it to win it!

Step 2: Pay Attention

Have you been burned dating men who *say* they're looking for the real deal but whose longest relationship is six months (or three weeks)? What about the guy who claims to be goal-oriented but spends most of his time watching sports or surfing the net when he should be pursuing those goals? The second step in dating smarter is to acknowledge that from now on, actions really do speak louder than words. Pay attention not only to what your potential dates are saying but *how* they're saying it, and then examine how their actions back up—or don't—those words.

And just as you should pay attention to your dates' behavior, you should also monitor your own actions. How? By really looking at the type of guy you're attracted to and/or attracting. If you're interested in settling down, chances are you don't want to pursue that young hottie at work who flirts with you by day, parties every night, and usually comes to work late (and hung over). And if you're just looking for some flirting fun, you should make your intentions known to that nice, sweet, stable guy who keeps calling and e-mailing with the hopes of taking you out for a romantic dinner. He may be okay with your casual dating manifesto, or he may want to cut his losses and look for someone as relationship-oriented as he is. If your new guy talks about wanting to settle down but can't seem to pay his bills on time, barely makes an effort to call you during the week, and always reserves Saturday night for his boys, his actions are definitely speaking louder than his words. Kick him to the curb and move on (unless you, too, are just looking for something casual).

> ## movin' on secret #5
> Dating is a two-way street. Just as it's not fair for some guy to string you along, it's equally unfair to bait a boy who's looking for love when you're not.

Step 3: Learn Your Lessons

In the past, did your dating life evoke a "been there, done that" feeling? Chances are if you're experiencing a dating déjà vu, there's probably a very good reason for it. Instead of ignoring that sinking sensation, *learn* from it. If your last boyfriend had a substance abuse problem, or a wandering eye, or workaholic tendencies, or commitment issues that made your relationship suffer and you're getting that *here we go again* feeling, listen to your gut. Of course, first be sure you're not dragging any stale emotional baggage around with you that just might be making you paranoid. *Then* trust your instincts and, if necessary, walk away.

As the keeper of your healed heart, you owe it to yourself to learn from past relationships. Once you've applied those hard-earned lessons, you'll be able to quickly and clearly identify those relationship red flags you want to avoid, and that means you're no longer doomed to repeatedly stumble over the same dating potholes time and again. *Hallelujah!*

AND SPEAKING OF DATING DÉJÀ VU

Have you identified the possible relationship potholes you repeatedly stumble over? Whether you have self-defeating notions about love, or you are attracted to guys who will never meet your emotional needs, or you somehow think you are inherently unworthy of love, it's these relationship ruts that you will continually run into until you identify and make peace with them. Keep your eyes peeled and your ears perked for your potential pitfalls and together, we'll figure out how to learn your lessons and move on.

In my own dating past, also known as my late twenties and early thirties, I found that I kept dating younger guys who were tons of fun but never quite ready to have a committed relationship with anyone but their bartender or buddies. As a result, I decided to stop dating men under the age of thirty. Imagine my surprise when the guys I dated who were my own age and older turned out to be equally commitment-phobic! I realized that I probably needed to take a look at the type of person I was attracted to and attracting. In doing so, I discovered that I gravitated toward the life-of-the-party type of guy. You know the ones. They laugh the loudest, have the most fun, and everyone wants to be their friend. And while these guys are always tons of fun to date, they are rarely (or in my case, never) emotionally equipped for a serious, stable long-term relationship.

Eventually, I came to the conclusion that I either had to change my expectations of these guys or redefine the type of partner I was looking for. I also had to ask myself why I thought I wanted to be with a man who everyone loved but who could never love me as much as he loved the spotlight. After some much-needed self-reflection, I faced the cold, hard truth that I had some self-esteem issues to work through. I took a break from dating, healed those internal issues, and eventually emerged as a healthy, happy, whole individual who just happened to be *single and ready to mingle*.

Taking the time to work on myself was the best thing I could have done for my healing heart. It allowed me to refocus my efforts and reprioritize what I was looking for in a relationship. Sure, I wanted to be with someone fun, but I came to understand that it was more important for me to find someone intelligent, grounded, emotionally available, and looking for love. In revisiting what I wanted from a relationship, I finally learned my lessons and started attracting more suitable suitors, some of whom were not only incredibly fun but smart, together, and driven.

Another benefit of doing my homework, identifying my relationship ruts, and learning my breakup lessons was that once I started attracting men who could meet my emotional needs, I found dating to be that much more enjoyable. Once you've identified and resolved your own relationship ruts, you will, too. Not only that, you may just meet someone amazing! In the meantime, if you're experiencing a dating déjà vu that's prodding you to run for the hills, trust your instincts and make that hasty retreat. By doing your homework and paying attention, you'll save yourself a lot of time and energy (and even possibly heartache).

Step 4: Date Yourself

Having trouble finding that perfect partner who's well suited for you? Your romantic challenges may have nothing to do with scarcity issues and everything to do with the fact that you have no idea what you should be looking for in a mate. The best way to figure out who might be right for you? Find out more about *You*! It may seem like a no-brainer, but knowing who you are and what you have to offer will help shape who and what you're looking for in a partner.

DATING TIP: MEN ARE LIKE SHOES

As you date, it's not so important *when* you settle down as it is that you settle down with the right guy. For many of us, that means dating—and trying on—lots of potential partners. Instead of beating yourself up for oh-so-many breakups, why not give yourself permission to audition as many guys for as long as it takes to find the perfect fit? (And don't settle for that partner who pinches your toes or slips in the heel. Keep looking until you find a comfortable, natural fit.)

Think back to the issues, ideas, and topics tackled in the last few chapters. It's been all about getting back to the business of you. Not only is it important to celebrate you and your fabulous life right now, but in doing so you're getting a clearer picture of who might be right to share that amazing life with you. By figuring out whether you're a homebody or a social butterfly, a conservative risk-taker or always open to new ideas, and then identifying the personality traits and qualities that are most important to you, you define and refine that picture of your perfect partner based on who *You* really are. And that will ultimately make for your most successful relationship ever. By the way, now is a good time to go back and review that list you made in Chapter 7 of traits you hope to find in your perfect partner. In fact, keep adding to it as you continue in Movin' On mode.

Step 5: Retrain Your Brain

Do you have self-defeating thoughts about dating, relationships, and/or love? Before you can really put yourself out there and attract healthy, happy, whole individuals, you first have to be healthy, happy, and whole on your own. That means letting go of any destructive ideas or notions about love and relationships that no longer work for you.

How do you do that? By retraining your brain. Don't worry, it's not as challenging as it sounds (no lobotomy required!). You just need to work on reframing your negative notions into positive ones, and in the process break up with those lingering bad love habits. First, take a look at some of the most commonly held negative relationship beliefs that follow. See if any of these resonate with you:

○ Do you blame your past relationship failures on your parents' good or bad marriage?
○ Do you believe there are no "good men" left?
○ Do you subscribe to the notion that love has to be difficult, painful, and/or challenging?
○ Are you convinced that you're a failure when it comes to love and relationships?
○ Are you hung up on someone or something from your past?
○ Do you think there is something inherently unlovable about you (such as debt, cellulite, crappy job, extreme shyness, overbearing parent, screwed up sibling, health problem, and so on)?

If you answered yes to any of the questions above, you may need to retrain your brain before you can become your most fabulous *single and ready to mingle* self. The first step is to identify your negative belief(s). The next step is to reframe the negative with a positive. For example, if you think love has to be difficult and painful, spend a few minutes every morning and evening repeating a mantra that replaces your self-defeating thoughts with healthier ones, like this one: "Love is here. Love is real. Love is unconditional. Love is available." Of course, how you complete the "Love is . . . " sentence is entirely up to you. Use words that are meaningful to you and replace your negative vocabulary with a positive one. Repeat this exercise every day for at least thirty days (or longer) until you really and truly believe your new vocabulary.

If you subscribe to the notion that there are no good men left, then you need to put the scarcity exercise from page 178 into practice. Every day, find ways in your routine to talk to one man you don't know. Be smart about who, when, and how you approach them. For example, don't strike up a conversation with a stranger in a parking garage at night or anywhere else you might feel unsafe and/or vulnerable. Instead, focus your efforts on highly populated places like your neighborhood farmers' market, the line for the Sunday matinee (or Wednesday night art film), on the way in or out the door of your yoga class, or in the elevator at your office building.

Keep in mind that the purpose of this exercise is not for you to make a love connection in five minutes or less. Rather, you just need to get in the habit of making casual connections with the opposite sex on a daily basis so you can see that not only are men *not* scarce, they're actually everywhere you go! Repeat the scarcity exercise every day for a month and see if that changes how you feel about men and/or your chances of meeting Mr. Right. (If you're particularly shy, see if this exercise boosts your confidence. I'm guessing that within thirty days, you'll feel a bolder *You* emerging!)

DATING TIP: DON'T FEAR REJECTION

Afraid to approach guys for fear they'll reject you? Unlike that grade-school bully we all lived in fear of, modern-day men are nowhere near as intimidating. In fact, you will most likely not get blatantly, horribly rejected by anyone you approach. Even if the guy is unavailable or uninterested, he will no doubt be flattered by your efforts and treat you nicely.

If you happen to think there is something inherently unlovable about you, you definitely need to retrain your brain. The truth is that each and every one of us deserves to love and be loved for exactly who we are, flaws, neuroses, warts, and all. So instead of beating yourself up for being plus-sized, having a dysfunctional family, being in a bit of a financial mess, or having a health problem, take time every day to celebrate your good qualities. Remind yourself that you deserve to find love—not "someday," when your problems are solved, but *today,* as your life is right now (and then get back to work on living and loving your life as it is!).

Depending on how long you've held onto all of your self-defeating belief(s), retraining your brain may take some time. It's important to repeat these exercises as often as necessary. It's perfectly healthy to flirt with and date men while you're retraining your brain. Just be sure to cut them some slack when those defeating thoughts pop up.

Step 6: Get Out There

Once you've retrained your brain and embraced a healthier, happier, more holistic approach to dating and relationships, it's time to put the last step in dating smarter into action. It's now time for you to get out there, that is, place yourself in target-rich environments whenever possible. And I don't just mean trolling every online dating site you can find. Sure, posting your online profile and some cute pics will aid your dating efforts. But as helpful as the Internet can be in your *single and ready to mingle* search, it's equally important to get out from behind that computer screen and make connections in the real world. If that sounds impossible, it's not. It may mean you have to shake up your routine a little, especially if your daily routine goes something like this—*home, work, gym, home, repeat.*

RECOVERY ℞

Hit a momentary setback in your celebratory single gal mode? Organize a girls' day out with your Woo-Hoo Crew complete with brunch, window shopping, and at least one hour spent in the target-rich environment of your choice.

The following is a week's worth of places to go and ways to get out there in hopes of meeting like-minded *single and ready to mingle* men no matter what the day, time, and/or season.

MONDAY

Recruit a fellow single gal from work or a girlfriend who works near you and take a long lunch at a target-rich location close by (whether that's a park bench, a popular eatery, or somewhere in between is up to you). Make eye contact with at least one handsome hottie and flash your pearly whites. Or act as a wing girl for your friend by making a casual introduction and then excusing yourself to the restroom so they can chat. (You can even take turns being each other's wing girls!)

TUESDAY

After work, stop by the bookstore in your most bootylicious jeans and hang out in the travel section. Flip your hair and smile at the cutie who's flipping through one of the Lonely Planet guides. Or leaf through your fave magazine at the newsstand and occasionally shoot that shy guy reading *Newsweek*, *Wired*, or *Atlantic Monthly* a friendly (or flirty) smile.

WEDNESDAY

If you're a pet owner, drop by your neighborhood pet supply store instead of just buying your cat or dog food at the grocery store. If you've got a dog, take your pooch to the dog park after work. If you're not a pet owner but like dogs, recruit your girlfriend with the beagle, bulldog, or retriever and together scope out the singles scene at the pet store or dog park. There's safety and strength in numbers!

THURSDAY

Drop by your neighborhood wine store and spend some time perusing the aisles. Ask the handsome man picking up a bottle of merlot about the wine he chose and/or if he has any wine suggestions for your upcoming dinner party (real or imagined—it doesn't matter!). If you don't drink, stop by your local hardware store or Home Depot. Ask the cutie in the carpentry aisle a question, or make eye contact with the nice-looking guy in the power tools section. Eye contact, a smile, and/or a casual question can spark a great first conversation!

FRIDAY

Peruse the local paper's events section to find out what's happening around your town. Then recruit your Woo-Hoo Crew for a fun evening of cocktails, art appreciation, open mike night, or any other activity/event that's sure to be target-rich. (And be sure to be each other's wing girls, as needed!)

SATURDAY

Go to Starbucks (or your favorite local coffee place) looking like a million bucks instead of in sweats and unwashed hair. Rather than order your coffee to go, bring a book, your iPod, your laptop (or girlfriends), and enjoy your beverage while scoping out the singles scene. (I've met many a man while waiting in line for my vanilla latte!)

SUNDAY

If you take your clothes to the neighborhood Laundromat, don't spend your downtime chatting on your cell phone with friends in your ratty T-shirt and cutoff shorts. Wear something casual and cute and strike up a conversation with the nice-looking guy who's waiting for his dryer to ding (bring a book, magazine, or notebook to make your mission less obvious and more enjoyable in case there are no cuties around).

Secret Strategies of the Numbers Game

Now that you know how to date smarter, you're ready to further maximize your success by incorporating the following secret strategies of the numbers game.

Play to Your Strengths

You don't have to change your personality to play the numbers game. Instead, you should play to your strengths. If you're outgoing, celebrate your bubbly personality by learning to *really* work a room. And if you love to flirt, get your flirt on whenever the opportunity arises! And if you happen to be shy? No problem! Use it to your advantage. Shoot that cutie across the room a shy smile, make eye contact, and then avert your gaze. Repeat this several times and see if that cutie doesn't take the hint and come across the room to meet you. Or recruit a friend to be your wing girl. (There's nothing wrong with asking for help if you're shy.) The key to playing the numbers game is not to be somebody you're not, but to be the best *You* possible.

Work the System

Because dating *is* a numbers game, it's up to you to work the system. That means not only putting yourself out there, but *circulating*. If you're at a singles event, cocktail party, or in any other target-rich environment, don't wait for *some guy* to approach you. Approach him. (And him. And him.) Strike up a casual conversation. Smile. Flirt! You're not going to find Mr. Right by standing in a corner waiting for him to find you (although you may get approached by Mr. Creepy, Mr. Pushy, and/or Mr. Misogynist). It's up to you to talk to as many potential candidates as possible until you find someone you really click with. That may take some time and energy, so get plenty of beauty rest and always keep a protein bar in your purse for those times when your fabulousness gets depleted by run ins with one too many Mr. Wrongs!

Define and Refine "Target-Rich"

Not only should you play to your strengths and put yourself out there, you should also make sure you're putting yourself out there in the right target-rich environments. If you want to meet a SNAG (sensitive new age guy) or other artsy creative type, don't waste your efforts hanging out at sports bars, Toby Keith concerts, or casting calls for *The Apprentice*. If religion's important to you, focus your efforts on church functions and/or join a spiritual singles group. And if you like buttoned-up preppy guys, then cross off goth clubs, rockabilly concerts, and tattoo parlors from your list of possible target-rich environments.

Always Be Prepared

Smart *single and ready to mingle* females should take a cue from the Boy Scouts and always be prepared. That means celebrating what makes you uniquely you, and putting your best *You* out there at all times. If you seriously want to play the numbers game, then every time you leave your house you should be in game mode. And no, that doesn't mean wearing makeup to the gym or 3-inch heels to pick up your dry cleaning. It just means that instead of running your weekend errands in sloppy sweats and unwashed hair, you might throw your hair in a ponytail or under a cute hat, wear something comfy but slightly adorable, and *pay attention* to your surroundings. You never know who you might meet if you make a little eye contact or share an inviting smile!

Play to Win

Because dating and the search for Mr. Right is a numbers game, you've got to have a winning strategy. Don't give up every time your efforts fall short. Of course there are going to be times when you get frustrated with your progress, fall into a momentary slump, and/or get discouraged. Take a short break (or breaks) as needed. But don't quit the game. Instead, treat it like you would your search for the perfect job or your quest for those strappy sandals you've been dreaming of. Keep looking until you find exactly what you've been searching for!

Conversation Starters

Now that you know how to date smarter and which target-rich environments to tackle, you need to have an opening line or two ready for when you casually bump into a potential cutie. The following are great conversation starters for almost any occasion.

In Line or in an Elevator

○ Compliment him on his watch, tie, shoes, or anything else about him that catches your eye.

○ Ask him what time it is, then smile, make eye contact, and say thanks when he tells you.

○ Just smile and say hi.

At a Bar or Lounge

○ If there's a game on television, ask who's playing and what the score is.

○ If there's live music, comment on something you like about the music (and then ask him what he thinks).

○ If there's canned music playing, ask him if he knows the name of the song, mention that you like the song, or make a joke about how cheesy the song is (depending on the song).

○ Or just smile and say hi.

At the Gym

○ If he's on a machine you want to use, ask him how much longer he'll be or ask him to show you how to use the machine when he's done.

○ If you're in a group exercise class, try to exit at the same time at the end of class and comment on what a great workout it was, how much you like the instructor, and so on.

○ Or, again, just smile and say hi.

When in doubt, remember that making conversation isn't rocket science. All you're really trying to do is initiate the beginning of a conversation and then see what unfolds. Your opening line doesn't have to be a winner; it just has to be a start. Once you've done that, you are then free to be your most charming and fabulous self!

Even if some of the men you meet are attached, or the interactions lead nowhere, it's still great practice to get comfortable striking up conversations with members of the opposite sex. If those guys ask for your name or number, all the better! Of course, only give out your number if you want to and feel comfortable doing so. You can always exchange e-mail addresses first or ask for his number instead.

DATING TIP: HE *COULD* BE INTO YOU

While there's validity in the whole *he's just not that into you* approach to dating, it's not as black-and-white as you may think. Sometimes guys just need a little encouragement. They may need to know you're interested. Give them the benefit of the doubt by making eye contact, smiling, and starting the conversation. If they don't respond, chalk it up to the fact that they probably weren't into you and move on. Until then, cut those shy cuties some slack!

As you continue in Movin' On mode, keep in mind that the art of conversation is not dead—so strike up some rich ones. You never know who you'll meet. If nothing else, your time at the bookstore, waiting for your laundry, or picking up more cat food will go that much faster (and you will have done yourself a favor in actively playing the numbers game!).

Breaking Up with Bad Love Habits

By following the six steps to dating smarter, identifying the target-rich environments that work for you, and getting more comfortable striking up conversations with cuties, your relationship future will be that much more enjoyable. However, our work isn't quite done. In reading through the six steps, did you identify any destructive beliefs about love and/or bad love habits that you may be holding onto?

Maybe you're attracted to bad boys who will never meet your needs, enjoy the thrill of the chase more than the joy of a relationship, or think that love is somehow unattainable for you. It's these self-defeating beliefs that may ultimately be keeping you from that healthy relationship you deserve. In order to kick these bad love habits, you've gotta do your homework by reviewing the six steps to dating smarter until you really and truly are living and loving yourself and your fabulous life. After all, as the keeper of your healed heart, you owe it to yourself to put those hard-earned breakup lessons into practice by paying attention, identifying relationship red flags and moving on from them, and reframing any negative beliefs about love and relationships. If you need help, visit me at *www.LisaSteadman.com*, where you'll find more information on how to become ready for a healthy and happy dating future, which is what you and your healed heart deserve.

Before we pat ourselves on the back and jump into dating with both feet, we've got one more hurdle to overcome. Can you guess what that might be? The next order of business in the fabulous female's guide to dating is to identify the bad boys in your life. We all have them—the guys we fall for too fast, the ones who constantly disappoint us, and who are ultimately bad for our emotional well-being. Sound familiar? Let's take a look at the boys to avoid in your dating future.

Boys to Avoid

The Addict He may like you or even love you, but the addict in your life will always love his addiction more. Whether he's a pothead, an alcoholic, or addicted to something more sinister is beside the point. What matters most is that he's got a problem, and it's not up to you to fix it or save him. As the keeper of your heart, you now know better. Walk away from this ticking time bomb. Just walk away.

The Control Freak At first, the control freak may be charming. He may woo you, wine you, dine you, sixty-nine you. But when his true colors emerge, there is no denying how ugly and *un*charming he really is. Whether he's telling you how to act, what to do, criticizing your actions, or belittling your behavior, you need to run—not walk—away from the control freak.

The Ladies' Man A show of hands—how many of us have fallen for the ladies' man at one time or another? He's smooth, charming, fun, and downright sexy. And once upon a time, maybe we thought he'd change his ways for us. But as the keeper of our healed heart, we now know better. Yes, the ladies' man is fun to flirt with or have a casual fling with, but he's not someone to trust our heart with or pursue when we're looking for a partner.

The Slacker The laid-back attitude, the sly smile, those fun lazy days spent hanging out without a care in the world all make the slacker absolutely adorable. And sure, when we were younger there was still the possibility that the slacker would snap out of his unambitious ways, get a real job and a 401(k) plan, and become our perfect life partner. But those days are long gone and for the sake of our healed heart, we gotta say *sayonara* to the slacker in our life.

The Victim Any guy who clings to his emotional baggage like it's the only thing keeping him above water is just bad news, especially for a *single and ready to mingle* gal who's done her homework and is traveling baggage-light these days. Whereas once upon a time, we might have thought we needed to save the victim in our life, we should now know better. It's not up to us to fix or save anyone. So make like the gingerbread man and run, run as fast as you can away from the victim.

The Workaholic Yes, your man should like what he does for a living. But if he's married to his job, he'll never be able to commit to you. Whether he puts in crazy long hours, brings work home with him at night and on weekends, or stays connected to the office 24/7 courtesy of his Blackberry, laptop, and/or cell phone, do yourself a huge favor and walk away from the workaholic. He will never have room for a full-time relationship *and* his demanding job, and you don't deserve to play second fiddle to a paycheck.

In looking at the boys to avoid in your dating future, did you have flashbacks to your dating past? I know I did! As someone who used to fall for guys with potential but too many issues, I think I've pretty much dated each guy on the above list. That's just fine because it's all in my past, which is hopefully where you'll keep your own boys to avoid.

See, it's one thing when we don't know any better. But once you identify the kind(s) of men you should definitely *not* date, you owe it to yourself to steer clear of them permanently and seek out only those suitors who are worthy of your time, energy, and general fabulousness. When in doubt, think about this. Neither myself nor any of my girlfriends has ever met an addict, control freak, or ladies' man who changed his ways for the woman in his life. That's not to say it can't be done or that it won't happen. But rather than waste your time praying for a miracle with the wrong guy, why not increase your odds of *happily ever after* by focusing on someone better suited for you (and in the meantime celebrating your saucy single self)?

In Defense of Nice Guys

In the past, you may have thought nice guys were too, well, *nice.* Dull, even. But as you relinquish your need for relationship drama, it's time to once again give nice guys a try. *But,* you may be wondering, *where do I find that nice guy?* Contrary to what you might think, they're not hiding out in their parents' basement or trapped under something heavy. Nice guys are everywhere—from the bike path to the chair lift to the sushi bar to your salsa dance class. While they may be less boisterous and not as attention-seeking as their bad-boy counterparts, they *are* out there, and they just may be waiting for someone as fun and fabulous as you to come into their lives. Think about it. Nice guys have been blown off for bad boys ever since Elvis first gyrated his pelvis. Nice guys would love to meet you, but they may just need a little encouragement from you in the form of eye contact, a welcoming smile, or a friendly "Hi." (Go for it!)

If you still think nice guys are a little on the boring side, take a look at the top ten reasons to give nice guys a try.

The Benefits of Dating a Nice Guy

1. Nice guys call when they say they're going to.
2. Nice guys are interested in you and your amazing life (and don't only talk about themselves!).
3. Nice guys like women and will treat you with respect.
4. Nice guys can be fantastic kissers.
5. Nice guys plan for the future (and may be looking to share it with someone like you!).
6. Nice guys make great boyfriends and husbands.
7. Nice guys make phenomenal fathers.
8. Nice guys care about your feelings.

9. Nice guys have passion (it just may be lurking below the surface).

10. Nice guys let you finish first (*Hallelujah!*).

If you remain unconvinced, you should go back and review the six steps to dating smarter. And if you're ready to give that nice guy a try, go for it!

So there you have it—the fabulous female's guide to dating. Learn it, love it, live by it. As the keeper of your healed heart, you are now armed with all the knowledge you need to date smarter and have a more fun and fulfilling dating future. May you never again get sidetracked by one of the boys to avoid, and when you're ready, may you find that nice guy of your dreams. In the meantime, enjoy playing the numbers game in as many target-rich environments as possible.

between-chapter *check-in*

Congratulations! After reading the last chapter, you're most likely feeling better equipped for a smarter dating future. You've hopefully also been able to identify any lingering bad love habits or hangups you may have been holding onto. Below or in your journal, I want you to write down at least one bad love habit or hangup that you're willing to release. Additionally, I want you to identify the most dangerous type of boy from your past that, as the keeper of your healed heart, you now promise to avoid.

Example: *After reading the chapter, I realize that I think love has to be hard. Based on my past experiences, I hold on to the idea that drama is a good thing. It's not, and I want to work on retraining my brain. As for the biggest bad boy in my past, I have a history of being attracted to workaholics. That's always caused problems in my relationships and from now on, I'm going to do my best to avoid any guy who's already married to his job. Buh-bye!*

DATE ☐ _____

_____

_____

_____

_____

CHAPTER TEN

wakeUP, breakUP, MOVE ON

at the very beginning of this book, I promised you something—that you would not only survive your Big Breakup, but that you would eventually thrive. And that you would one day wake up and say *Thank God!* for the one who got away. Has that day arrived yet? If not, don't worry. It's on its way.

If not today, then one day in the not-too-distant future you will be minding your own business, actively involved in your amazing life, and a familiar song will come on the radio. Or you'll be flipping through the channels and that movie, television show, or commercial will just happen to be on that used to be a painful reminder of Mr. Ex. But on this particular day, the pain will have subsided to the point where you'll smile, feel a sense of peace, and give thanks that Mr. Ex is no longer in your life. Then you will get on with your day, armed with the knowledge that you have successfully survived and thrived. At this point, I once again remind you . . .

"*congratulations* on your breakup!!!"

And more importantly . . .

"*congratulations* on movin' on!!!"

Whether you know it or not, you have just graduated in a way. Yes you, my fabulous friend, really are the hero of your amazing life. You are now a bona fide breakup recovery rock star who deserves to live and love her life because you've done the work, put in the time, and are now well on your way to *happily ever after*. What you choose to do from here on out is up to you (and your destiny may still be unfolding as we speak). In the meantime, let's review a few last-minute lessons to help make the journey that much sweeter.

Last-Minute Lessons

Just like after your Big Breakup and throughout your Movin' On recovery, you will have ups and downs along the road to *happily ever after*. That's perfectly normal. Life, after all, is not always sunshine and roses. You may have moments when you doubt your progress and days when you'll question your sanity. There will even be times when you'll just get tired of being your sensational *single and ready to mingle* self. If and when you find yourself faltering, don't give up. Accept the momentary setback for being what it is—momentary. If needed, take a break from whatever's overwhelming you for some much-needed cocoon time. Rest, recoup, refuel. When you're ready, pick yourself up, dust yourself off, and get back out there as the bold and beautiful butterfly that you are.

The Road to Happily Ever After

If the last chapter prepared you for a smarter and more successful dating future, this chapter is a reminder that you should never give up in your search for *happily ever after*, whatever form that may take in your own life. If what you truly want is a loving relationship with your perfect partner, then that's going to take some time to find. Now that you're better prepared to date smarter (thanks in part to knowing yourself better and identifying the boys you need to avoid), you're sure to find romantic success.

As you begin to date smarter, you will most likely find yourself in the company of some really great guys. Some will be short-lived relationships that serve as gentle nudges in new dating directions, like the great guy who spends a little too much of your time together talking about himself. He'll help you realize you want someone more down-to-earth. Or the great divorcee who for whatever reason has a kid he never sees. He may nudge you to keep looking for a guy who will one day be a fantastic father for your future kids.

And then you will date other great guys who may seem pretty perfect for you. You may even be able to see yourself with them over the long term. They may *almost* be The One. How fabulous is that? As the keeper of your healed heart, you're doing everything right. You're trusting your gut, selecting only appropriate and available candidates and further refining what you're looking for in your perfect partner. Ultimately, only you will know if these great guys are the great guy for you or if they're just one of the many great guys along your journey toward *happily ever after.*

Once I started dating smarter, I dated a lot of really great guys. And along the way, I encountered a handful of *almost* perfect partners. We shared common interests, had similar senses of humor, and genuinely enjoyed each other's company. While there was nothing particularly wrong with any of them, none of these guys was quite right for me. Whether it was timing, chemistry, or just a nagging feeling in my gut, something always told me that this was not the guy to give my heart to. And as the keeper of my healed heart, it was my job to listen to and honor that command.

As time went on, I began to trust that inner voice completely. It never led me astray. In fact, it led me to my perfect partner, Mr. XY. Once you tune in to your own inner voice, you will never be led astray either. In doing your homework, you just may find your very own Mr. XY. (In fact, I bet you will!)

Troubleshooting Happily Ever After

"I *just knew* he was The One."

Throughout my *single and ready to mingle* years, I can't tell you how many times I heard those words from a recently engaged or married friend or acquaintance. And to be honest, I always found it infuriating. Not to mention a little condescending. Never having had that feeling, at least not accompanied by "Well, at least I *hope* he's The One," hearing someone else say those words made me feel like a failure in the relationship department. What was wrong with me that I didn't *just know* when someone was The One? Was I too complicated? Screwed up? Damaged goods? Of course not. And neither are you.

The truth is, when the right guy comes along you may or may not *just know*. I've had girlfriends who hated their husband when they first met him. Or maybe they initially thought their future husbands were too nice, too normal, too tame for them. As for me, when I met Mr. XY, I wasn't even paying attention to whether or not he might be The One. We met casually one Saturday night. When he asked for my number as he and his friends were leaving later that evening, I gave it to him without a second thought. And when he called the next day and asked me to dinner, I agreed.

Still, I wasn't thinking about where this might be going or if he was in fact The One for me. Sure, I thought he was nice, a great conversationalist, and kinda cute. But I also thought he was too young, too conservative, too traditional for me. And when he showed up on my doorstep for our first date in a preppy blue sweater, dress slacks, and polished shoes with a bouquet of spring flowers in one hand, well, I wondered why I was wasting this poor guy's time.

But about halfway through dinner, somewhere between our conversation about why I left my safe, stable corporate job to pursue relationship writing (with him nodding in understanding as I talked about following my dreams) and him telling me about his trip to Paris last Christmas (with me nodding as he talked about how he *just knew* if he didn't go, he'd regret it), I realized something. There was more to Mr. XY than met the eye. Underneath the preppy exterior and impeccable manners lay a thoughtful, passionate, inspired human being. Those usually noisy voices in my head that regularly pointed out relationship red flags and alerted me to potential pitfalls suddenly went silent. And the only voice left said, *You should give this guy a chance.* So I sat back, listened, and allowed myself to get to know Mr. XY. But even then, I wouldn't say I *just knew.*

When the right guy comes along for you, maybe you'll *just know.* But don't beat yourself up if you don't. It doesn't mean that the great guy sitting across from you doesn't have potential to be The One. It may just take time to come to you. In my case, I never had a trumpets-blaring, fireworks-bursting, *I-just-knew* kind of moment.

REVISITING YOUR FABULOUS FACTOR

As a way of paying tribute to all that you've been through, it's time to once again revisit your Fabulous Factor list. How does it make you feel? Like you've come a long way since you first started that list? You have! And today's the day to celebrate that fact. It's also the day to write down at least one more fabulous thing about yourself. It can relate to your recovery or just be something fabulous you've recently discovered. So go ahead. Add at least one more thing to your list.

The closest I came was on my third date with Mr. XY, when I walked up the stairs to his apartment where he was waiting to cook me dinner. Suddenly, I had this overwhelming feeling that I was standing on the edge of a cliff. Below me was the future. I was pretty sure it was a future that involved Mr. XY. But at that moment, walking up those stairs, I remained uncertain. Was I ready to go there again? Was I ready to risk everything I'd worked so hard to reconstruct after my Big Breakup? And most importantly, did I think my healed heart would be safe with Mr. XY? As scared as I was, my gut told me it would be okay. And maybe in that moment I *just knew* because I decided to take the leap.

For the first time in a long time, I gave myself permission to open my heart. It was a risk, but I'd done my homework, waited for a guy who I felt was deserving of my love, and as the keeper of my healed heart, I'd chosen wisely. And so will you. But don't take my word for it. I don't want to be one of those infuriatingly condescending *I just knew* kind of chicks. Trust yourself and your healed heart. You'll know when it's right. You'll know when you're ready to risk it all for the right person, someone who's worth all that hard work you've been doing along the way. In the meantime? Just keep going. And never forget to live and love your life as it is right now. You've earned it. It's time to reap the rewards of successfully surviving your Big Breakup and thriving in Movin' On mode!

Finding Your Perfect Partner

We all know that nobody's perfect, right? And yet we bend over backwards to find our perfect partner in life, often frustrating ourselves in the process because we meet so many imperfect people. Our efforts are further thwarted by those childhood fairy tales promising a white knight on a white stallion or a dashing prince who will sweep in and save the day when what we usually meet in our everyday lives are nothing but horny toads and unkissable frogs. (At least that's how it sometimes seems.)

The truth is that nobody's perfect. There is no prince. Like it or not, nobody's coming along to rescue you or take you away from your everyday grind. That's why it's so important to create a life that you live and love on your own terms—so that when your perfect partner does come along and his front tooth is crooked, or he's shorter than you imagined, or his student loan debt is as staggering as yours is, you'll still recognize him for the amazing individual that he is. You'll still give him the time of day because you know that while he's far from perfect, he's pretty perfect for you. Maybe he's too young, too old, drives a crappy car, or has a crappy job. But more importantly, maybe he makes you laugh. Or meets your needs. Or just "gets" you. And that's what makes him so perfect for you, warts and all. It's up to you to give this great guy a chance. When the right one comes along, whether you *just know* it or not, you owe it to yourself to take a chance and open your heart.

Now that you're well on your way toward *happily ever after*, it's time to celebrate! Get out your journal and revisit your life list from Part One. Look it over and start adding new things. Remember, your life list will serve as a reminder from this day forward of who you are, who you want to become, and all the things you want to strive for as you live out your fabulous life. From *practice more patience* to *be a better friend* to *backpack through South America*, this is a list that will shape your future. Always hold on to it and keep adding to it! To make it more meaningful, invite your Woo-Hoo Crew over for cocktails and encourage each of your gal pals to make her own life list. Together, you can support and inspire one another to cross things off your lists on a regular basis. It's your life. Shouldn't you live it out loud and with purpose? (The answer's *yes!*)

A Final Word about Your Ex

Okay, I haven't mentioned your ex in quite a while, but before we get to *The End*, we have to once again open your ex file and tidy up some loose ends. In a perfect world, after a breakup our exes would either disappear from the face of the earth or shrivel up into wrinkled, sad, and lonely versions of their former selves. But because science has yet to perfect either of these scenarios, as it stands right now your ex is still allowed to roam free. And that means he probably has a life of his own. Like it or not, it may at one time or another (depending on the size of the city you share) intersect with your own fabulous life. Now, depending on how benevolent the universe is feeling when that happens, your ex encounter may be mild and feel like nothing more than that pinch on Saint Patty's Day when you forgot to wear green. Or it could be slightly more aggravating, like getting a speeding ticket when you're already running late for work. Or, if for some reason the universe is feeling particularly wicked that day, your ex encounter could feel like a swift kick to the gut.

In Part One of this book, I told you that time plus distance equaled moving on from your ex. And that was true. Your Movin' On recovery is proof of that. But that doesn't mean that you'll ever be fully prepared to re-encounter your ex. (My Big Breakup is three years old and I'm *still* not sure I'd be ready to see Mr. Ex.) The following is a preview of the best- and worst-case scenarios for re-encountering your ex. It's important to have a contingency plan in place should either scenario actually occur.

Best-Case Scenario

You've lost twenty pounds, got a big fat promotion and raise at work, and just got engaged to the man of your dreams. The two of you are locked in a passionate embrace when your ex walks by in wrinkled clothes, disheveled hair, and in the middle of an asthma attack. He's lost his job, his home, and his will to live. He sees you looking amazing. You see him looking, well, horrible. Or you're so consumed with passion for your new man that you don't even see the ex. Life is good. The universe is kind. And you are very, very lucky.

Should this scenario actually occur, here's your contingency plan. Take pity on your ex and ask if there's anything you can do to help. At least give him cab fare so he can get to the hospital and seek medical treatment for his breathing problems. (But first, be sure he gets a good look at the sparkler on your left hand. It may be petty, but it feels good to be this fabulous!)

Worst-Case Scenario

You're in a dating dry spell (or you just got dumped by some guy you didn't even like that much). Your new best friend is the kind-faced counter lady at Krispy Kreme. Your roots are showing, you've got massive cramps, and those dark circles under your eyes are more noticeable than ever. Not only that, but your purse was just stolen including your wallet, keys, and cell phone. You're walking down the street in tears when up ahead you see them. Your ex and his new supermodel girlfriend. They're holding hands, laughing, having the time of their lives. You make eye contact. And as they walk by, he pretends not to know you. It's then that you realize rock bottom was just the beginning. A crack of thunder roars, the sky opens up, and it begins to hail.

If this worst-case scenario should actually happen, here's your contingency plan. Fish your emergency $20 out of your Wonder bra (hey, you *are* still fabulous!), and grab a cab to your nearest Woo-Hoo Crew member's home. In no time, she'll have gathered the other girls, whipped up a batch of killer margaritas, and together you'll spend the evening commiserating and ultimately giving thanks that you let your ex get away. Before the night is over, one of your fab friends will remind you that dating a high-maintenance Amazon with an eating disorder is probably more tedious and time consuming than your ex's tiny pea brain or limited attention span can handle, and he's likely to get dumped at any moment.

Chances are neither of these scenarios will actually ever happen and your ex encounter will be much less dramatic (a random e-mail, an awkward phone call, a chance run-in). But it may still bring up residual resentment, a flushed flash-back, or other emotions you haven't felt in some time. That's okay!

As far as you've come and as much as you've learned, you're still human. You used to share a life with your ex. A re-encounter with him may make your heart pound. It may make you queasy. It may even make you doubt your sanity for a minute. But you know what? Give it another minute. You're going to be just fine. You've done your homework and learned those hard-earned breakup lessons. So regardless of how your ex re-encounter goes down, you, my fabulous and fearless friend, have broken *up* with that relationship that no longer worked and moved on to a life better suited for you. A life you now live and love. One that you are the amazing hero of.

Who cares if your ex has a new girlfriend, or a new job, or a new lease on life? Not you. You're far too fabulous to crane your neck to look at the past when your present and future are as spectacular as yours are! Yes, your ex may fall in love again before you do. He may get engaged, married, and/or have a baby before you do. But that doesn't mean he won. It's not a competition.

If your Big Breakup and subsequent Movin' On recovery have taught us anything, it's that your *happily ever after* has nothing to do with your ex. In fact, your *happily ever after* starts with you. It's something that comes from deep within. Sure, it may one day include a man, a ring, and possibly a baby, if that's what you truly desire. But in the meantime, it's up to you to find your inner *happily ever after* and celebrate it for all it's worth. And believe me, it's worth a lot. Welcome to the first day of the rest of your life, a life full of amazing adventures, should you choose them. And from the looks of it you already have.

(Good luck!!!)

end-of-book *check-in*

Congratulations! You have just successfully survived your Big Breakup and graduated from your Movin' On metamorphosis. How do you feel? Below or in your journal, write down a sentence or two describing how you feel at this very moment.

Example: *I am so proud of myself for going through the pain of my Big Breakup and embracing Movin' On mode. I rock!*

DATE [   ] _____

_____

_____

One final note: As you move on with your fabulous life, it's important to remember that it's not always going to be easy. From time to time, you will have setbacks in living and loving your life as it is right now. When you need to, revisit this book for a refresher course in whatever you're struggling with. You can also visit me at *www.LisaSteadman.com* where you'll find additional breakup, dating, and relationship resources, information on my coaching services, not to mention like-minded individuals on the message board. Above all else, remember this: Be patient with your progress. Give yourself cocoon time as needed. Then when you're ready, pick yourself up, dust yourself off, and get back in the game. In the meantime, give yourself a pat on the back for being such an amazing breakup recovery rock star!

Acknowledgments

By far, the easiest part about writing a book is the acknowledgments. This was such a collective effort, and I have many people to thank so, without further ado, here it goes. Mucho thanks to Jennifer Kushnier and all the folks at Adams Media for their support of my first book. I'm thrilled to have found a home at Adams! To Danielle Chiotti at Kensington Books, for developing this book with me and believing in it before anyone else did. To Kelly Bare, for giving my work a shot on TangoMag.com where I was *discovered*. To Caroline Levchuck, for giving me my start as a writer all those years ago, and being instrumental to so much of my success over the years. You have been an incredible mentor, coach, and fountain of knowledge. This book would not exist without you!

To my parents, who are both instrumental in who I am today. Mom, thank you for passing on your creativity to me and for our recent summers in Montana together. Dad, you always let me know that it was okay to be me, even if that meant I marched to a different drum than the rest of you. Thanks for raising me with the knowledge that I am my own person (and for setting such a good example). To my sister Staci, for always being there for me and supporting me and letting me be me. I am so lucky to have you as my sissy! To the amazing WishBox Writers, my creative family who has loved and supported me through the joys and pains of our creative lives together. Specifically to Andre, whose prolific talent and unique voice amaze me (*keep writing!*); to Anne, who is sure to be the next great American novelist; to

Karraine, our gifted moon goddess poet who has shown us all the way to live a freer creative life; and to Gretchen, who is the most genuinely creative person I know (and who will one day hit it *so big*!).

To my longtime friends: Lani, Allen, and Joe of Epiphanies, Inc. Lani, you are my soul sister and not a day goes by when I don't give thanks for you being in my life; to my true blue L.A. friends for all your love and support over the years—Jim, there are so many reasons to thank you but in terms of this book, thanks for turning me on to *Tango* in the first place and for helping me move after a breakup or two; to my fellow writer (and savvy single!) Mattie, who was my first published author friend and helped me realize it was possible; to Brett, who wrote with me that first day. I don't know how I could have started this book without you! To Leslie and the girls for your love and kindness; to Stef and Steve for food, fun, and game nights; to my hysterically hilarious hair genius (and friend) Chad, who has the most vivid imagination I've ever known; to Charlie, for years of friendship and support and shared dreams; to my Crafty Chris Varaste and Awesome Renee Dawson, for our magical summer together. Renee, thank you for introducing me to the man of my dreams. You are the best wing girl ever! Chris, thank you for your ongoing friendship, love, and for all your great advice when I was first dating Mr. XY; to Evie, Orio, and Izzybelly, who are just starting to live their dream life; to my fabulous girls around town—Negin, Debra, Melanie, Paula, Melinda, and Shona; to the Eagle family and my West Yellowstone, Montana, crew. Thank you for giving me a second home and welcoming me into your corner of the world.

To Ron Rosen, for being the most generous, hip, and decent lawyer I've ever met (and for believing in my book even though you've been happily married for decades!); and of course to Janice Mills, for being instrumental in my sister's and my lives for many years now. From condos to moral support to book deals, you are a true Rainmaker!

To Wendy Ray, who brought *The Breakup Chronicles* to life with her amazing design skills; to Alan Donnelly, for programming in a pinch and never overcharging me; to each and every person who has ever visited BreakupChronicles.com, submitted a story, and to everyone on my message board. You guys *rock*! To the makers of Dragon Naturally-Speaking® voice software for helping a girl with tendonitis achieve her dreams of writing her first book. There would be no book without your product. *Thank you*!

To three teachers who enriched my life and made me the writer I am today—Mrs. Germanson, for cramming grammar down my ninth-grade throat; Mr. Strayhorn, for coaxing the reluctant writer out from under my shy, bored, black-clad facade; and Chris Knopf, for giving me the best advice anyone ever has when he told me that dedication was just as important as talent, and I was lucky to be marginally blessed by both.

To all the Mr. Exes who have entered and exited my life over the years. I am a better person for having known each and every one of you. I wish you all health, happiness, and true love.

And finally, to the two men in my life who were most instrumental in making this book happen. To Scott, who believed in my breakup book idea long before anyone else did, and who helped coax the Web site, product line, and book into reality. Your exceptional talent, never-ending stream of ideas, and your ability to challenge me when I don't even know I need it have greatly contributed to our success. I am eternally grateful for your friendship, guidance, and advice.

And lastly, to Luis. You are my rock *and* you rock my world, a winning combination I never thought I'd find. Every day with you is a gift. Being your partner makes me feel like I'm the luckiest girl in the world. Your ongoing love, support, and partnership have greatly enriched not only my life but this book as well. I love you!

Index

about the author

Lisa Steadman, The Relationship Journalist™, studies breakups, dating, and relationships for a living. Her writing has appeared on iVillage.com, TangoMag .com, and MSN.com Lifestyle, among others, and her site *www.BreakupChronicles.com* features true-life tales of how breaking up the wrong person is the right thing to do. She lives in Los Angeles with her boyfriend whom she met after successfully surviving her Big Breakup and celebrating her *single and ready to mingle* self, using the tips and techniques she shares in this book.

more POLKA DOT press® titles

The 10 Women You'll Be Before You're 35
$12.95
ISBN 10: 1-59337-277-9
ISBN 13: 978-1-59337-277-4

Addickted
$14.95
ISBN 10: 1-59337-731-2
ISBN 13: 978-1-59337-731-1

Been There, Done That, Kept the Jewelry
$14.95
ISBN 10: 1-59337-635-9
ISBN 13: 978-1-59337-635-2

Better Off Wed?
$14.95
ISBN 10: 1-59337-347-3
ISBN 13: 978-1-59337-347-4

The Dating Cure
$14.95
ISBN 10: 1-59337-261-2
ISBN 13: 978-1-59337-261-3

Dating, Inc.
$14.95
ISBN 10: 1-59869-076-0
ISBN 13: 978-1-59869-076-7

It's a Breakup, Not a Breakdown
$14.95
ISBN 10: 1-59869-172-4
ISBN 13: 978-1-59869-172-6

Men at Work
$14.95
ISBN 10: 1-59337-495-X
ISBN 13: 978-1-59337-495-2

Read My Hips
$14.95
ISBN 10: 1-59337-456-9
ISBN 13: 978-1-59337-456-3

Sex With Your Ex
$12.95
ISBN 10: 1-59869-205-4
ISBN 13: 978-1-59869-205-1

Tales from the Scale
$12.95
ISBN 10: 1-59337-328-7
ISBN 13: 978-1-59337-328-3

The Thrifty Girl's Guide to Glamour
$14.95
ISBN 10: 1-59337-622-7
ISBN 13: 978-1-59337-622-2

Available wherever books are sold. Or call 1-800-258-0929 or visit us at *www.adamsmedia.com*.

www.LisaSteadman.com